P

The Analysis of Complex Socioeconomic Systems

The Analysis of Complex Socioeconomic Systems

Peter S. Albin
John Jay College, CUNY
and
New York University

Lexington Books
D.C. Heath and Company
Lexington, Massachusetts
Toronto   London

Library of Congress Cataloging in Publication Data

Albin, Peter S.
  The analysis of complex socioeconomic systems.

  Bibliography: p.
  Includes index.
  1. Social sciences—Methodology. 2. Social science research. I. Title.
H61.A53   300'.7'2   74-19860
ISBN 0-669-96636-3

Published simultaneously in Canada.

Printed in the United States of America.

International Standard Book Number: 0-669-96636-3

Library of Congress Catalog Card Number 74-19860

For Pat, John, and Nancy

Contents

List of Figures

List of Tables

Preface

My interest in the mathematical forms of automata and cellular automata began in 1971 when I was exposed to the "game of Life" (explained and demonstrated in Chapter 1), a fascinating mathematical recreation which was brought to popular attention by Martin Gardner in his *Scientific American* column. Like many others, I became an amateur of "Life" and carried out whimsical experiments with this highly visual automata format. My interest in automata as a serious research tool stemmed from the simple observation that "Life forms" could be made to behave like populations grouped into towns or villages and that similar forms could represent "capital goods" and other artifacts. What struck me was that in working with automata that derived from "Life," a very few operating principles generated model behaviors which seemed to be as interesting as those produced by quite massive constructions. In particular, one could work with physical relationships that harkened back to the classical period in economic analysis (i.e., a specific tool used by a specific worker, twelve plots of land worked by three families, and the like); and it seemed quite practical to separate the value side of economic activity from the technical side, and reintegrate them where appropriate. With a bit of ingenuity, one could combine the elements to form an intriguing world apparently filled with social interactions, threshold phenomena, environmental effects, and evolutionary or adaptive developments.

The first modeling experiments, although crude, were promising enough to attract me to a deeper examination of the foundation discipline. There are a number of distinct literatures on cellular automata, but I had the good fortune to begin formal study with the works of von Neumann and Burks (cited in the bibliography) rather than with the more systematic text developments in computer science and abstract algebra.[a]

Von Neumann's *Theory of Self-Reproducing Automata* is clearly the strongest intellectual influence on the present work. The book itself consists of a posthumous reconstruction based on working notes, sketches, constructive proofs, and related popular lectures. In one sense, the compilation records the manner in which a powerful intelligence organized empirical materials, insights, and metaphysical conjectures to develop an important proposition and to design its proof. In another sense, it is a store of conjectures on the potential use of a powerful organizing concept. Von Neumann's specification of threshold levels of complexity as a biological principle governing organization, his stress on

---

[a]The computer-science literature is, of course, directed to practical applications in machine design and programming while the abstract mathematical approach leads toward formal generalizations. Both produce specific results that can be useful for the social sciences, but specialization is far advanced and it is difficult to pick up the integrating links. Linguistic and neurophysiological applications also exist, but they seem to lack direct economic relevance.

structure in dynamic processes, and his style in heuristic analysis appear as distinct themes in distinct successor literatures, but to my knowledge they are integrated nowhere else but in his seminal work.

As far as the present study is concerned, the von Neumann approach suggested the simultaneous importance of three major themes: first, the usefulness of cellular-automata simulation methods in heuristic modeling; second, the possibility of formal analysis and measurement of complexity characteristics; and finally, the possibility of an entirely new class of propositions on system equilibrium and dynamic behavior which derive uniquely from viewing social systems as automata. It also became clear that these themes were cooperative in nature and could not be developed independently—that automata modeling of real-world systems could only really be advocated on evidence that the approach was linked to a new type of measurement and to insightful theory—that acceptance of a complexity-measurement approach clearly depended upon there being something to measure, while acceptance of theoretical propositions relied on some assurance that the forms used have some empirical base.

In short, the research program, as I originally saw it, involved proceeding simultaneously on the three fronts of simulation, complexity measurement, and pure theory. This program accounts for my research activity over the past few years, the plan of the book, and the expository style which fluctuates between formal mathematics, heuristics, and intuitive conjecture (as well as whimsy—a derivative of game of Life exposure).

The actual research was assisted by a number of institutions, including the Schools of Business Research Fund, the Institute of Applied Economics, and Institute of Labor Relations at New York University, and the Lawrence Radiation Laboratory at Berkeley. The various parts of the work were put together at New York University, the University of Cambridge, the University of California, and John Jay College. Seminars at these schools, at the National Bureau, at the Research Center for Economic Planning, and at the World Bank contributed to the development of the research. The author is indebted to these institutions and to Random House, Inc. for permission to reprint material from Jane Jacobs, *The Economy of Cities*, New York: Vintage Books, Random House, Inc., 1970.

On a more personal note, the simulation side of the research was advanced most by work with Austin Hoggatt at Berkeley, where Mike Katz and Craig Dore, two extraordinary computer science students, designed an effective and powerful model of a primitive economy that was a continuous source of insight. Speculative work on microsimulators was carried out at the Research Center for Economic Planning with Thomas Vietorisz, Bob Mier, and Bennett Harrison. (Professor Harrison developed an automaton simulator independently in his M.I.T. workshop, and results from his study are described later.) Toni Kamiko executed the diagrams, and Helen Ray completed the final typing of the manuscript while working on two books of her own.

There is a long list of individuals whose comments and criticisms contributed to this work. I recall in particular Roger Alcaly, William Baumol, George Bitros, John Eatwell, Geoff Heale, Janos Ordover on the economic side of the work; Alvy Smith, Jack Keller, Donald Ludwig on mathematical issues; and Walter Peters along with M. Richard Kirstell as willing listeners. When the major debts are calculated, however, I must acknowledge the intellectual support of Austin Hoggatt, Bruno Stein, and Tom Vietorisz. But that is, after all, what is meant by friendship.

Introduction

This book is methodological in tone and purpose but oriented to the economist and behavioral scientist rather than the pure mathematician or computer scientist. Involved is a technique "smallest unit representation" (henceforth abbreviated "SUR"), which is itself derived from the mathematical discipline variously labeled "cellular automata theory" (CA) or "theory of finite automata." The mathematical field originated in speculative work by von Neumann and S. Ullam and now stands as the foundation discipline in abstract computer science, linguistics, and mathematical logic. Applications abound, and the theory provides the basis for some remarkable advances in diverse life science fields, including cellular growth and organization, neural organization, and epidemiology. We shall see that the field offers unusual results and suggestive possibilities in the social sciences.

The essential motif in CA theory is that of representing a unit or component in a complex, interactive system as an automaton, a "black box" which is specified in terms of the states assumed by the unit and a few conventions and restrictions that describe timing and transitions. Combinatorial logic or computing power can be used to trace the behaviors of systems made up of such units or to analyze system structure. It frequently turns out that the automata closely resemble real-world counterparts, while the logic of their interactions corresponds closely to intuition. In such cases, one operates with a literal and direct image of the reference system—but an image, metaphor, or model that is susceptible to deep and rigorous analysis. This is surely true for existing applications in the computer or natural sciences and in linguistic studies. Abstract automata can correspond closely to mechanical components, biochemical body components, or language elements, and studies of the structure of systems made up of such components have been revealing.

Our concern will be with automata representation of socioeconomic systems; the representation of individuals as automata characterized by demographic, labor force, and class-state descriptions (corresponding to census categories); the representation of associations and institutions as ensembles of automata; and representation of machines, tools, artifacts, and commodities as distinct automata characterized according to state descriptions of the sort found in specifications handbooks or industrial censuses. The argument is that analysis of the structure of systems made up of such components can be insightful as to the essential nature of the referent elements and their interactions, and that important policy and positive findings will follow.

The argument is actually sharper than this. First, we will see that most of the standard quantitative models used by economists and behavioral scientists are in fact automata forms and can be analyzed as such. This in itself is a very minor revelation—comparable to that experienced by Moliere's *Bourgeois Gentilhomme* on discovering that what he had been speaking for forty years was prose. Economists have been communicating with automata language for forty years and more and have not needed to know the name of the language, its grammar and canons of style. This book intends to show that the use of the language can be enhanced by looking at just these aspects. The second part of the argument is the essential one, however. To reiterate: we will see that many economic agents, economic activities, and social relations in the real world are expressable as formal automata. Acting on this information, new models can be designed and existing model forms adapted to take advantage of results which are in the automata discipline, but not yet incorporated within the social sciences.

The transference of methodology is not without dangers; the success of a technique in one discipline offers no guarantee that it can be or should be transferred to another. Quantum mechanics and statistical mechanics both achieved commanding successes within the physical sciences in roughly the same period of time. But despite many efforts to transfer the methodology, the quantum model has had virtually no impact within the social sciences while techniques based on statistical mechanics have flourished. In light of this, CA-derived methodology should not be examined just because of successes within the originating disciplines—these simply suggest that the systematic mathematical development of the field is well advanced—but rather because the methodology gives immediate answers and promises of answers to recognized and substantial questions. This, we will argue, is the case. The SUR approach provides a practical working technique for modeling detailed socioeconomic relationships. In this mode, heuristic and policy applications abound. SUR also provides a theoretical method that gives immediate results on established problems in capital theory, but in the process suggests a family of novel conjectures which conform to intuition but have not been previously formalized. These are substantial claims, and it will be useful to examine their scope in some detail before proceeding to the actual analysis.

Issues of Simulation or Representation

Let us begin with a description of a number of problems which can be handled in the simulation mode. The SUR approach offers the following to applied economists and other social scientists:

1. A practical technique for computer representation of the explicit ways in which microbehavioral units (individuals, consumers, households, workers, etc.) interact with one another.

2. Practical techniques for computer representation of their interaction with means of production: plots of land, individual machines, factory systems, and complex chains of industry and distribution.
3. A locational framework in which production and social systems can be explicitly tied to place and to spatial organization.
4. A simulation approach which can make direct use of empirical data in the form of technical specifications, i.e., plot fertility, machine capacity, and other "catalog" specifications, physical capacity of an aged worker, etc.
5. A representation technique which can easily handle explicit ethnographic relationships such as taboos, patterns of discrimination, old-boy networks, and so on.
6. A system of simulation that can incorporate developmental sequences such as the passage from workshop to factory operation or from unorganized farmstead to agribusiness.
7. A system of simulation which can encompass threshold phenomena such as racial "tipping points" or critical levels of congestion or pollution (environmental flash points) or "critical masses" of educated personnel.

The list of simulation or representation possibilities could be extended. It should simply be noted at this time that the phenomena listed are frequently awkward to handle by conventional heuristic or analytical means, and many, despite their real-world significance, can only be handled in an ad hoc fashion. The SUR approach offers a discipline for heuristic modeling which is practical on modern computers, surprisingly easy to comprehend, yet rooted in hard and deep theory (the CA discipline). This theory proves to be readily transferable to the economic context and provides a basis for sensible monitoring of heuristic analysis.

Theoretical Issues

On its own the CA discipline suggests a collection of new and significant theorems at the foundations level in pure economics. Included are conjectures on the following matters:

1. The drawing up of measures of complexity so that one could, in practice, derive "objective" indices of degrees of organization and development; such indices could be used in cross-sectional comparisons (e.g., New York City versus Detroit, France versus Japan) or in historical assessments (e.g., analysis of productivity gains attributable to the higher degree of national integration possible with improved communication and transport).
2. The measurement of infrastructural and organizational requirements of industrial systems.
3. The effects of technical changes on such requirements.

4. Links between scale and the complexity dimension.
5. Alternate techniques for studying decomposability, autarky, and dependence.
6. Techniques for measurement of heterogeneous capital on a variety of value bases.
7. Capital and planning theories which take explicit account of traverses and out-of-equilibrium dynamic sequences.
8. The econometric characteristics of data which are generated by complex dynamic systems.
9. Practical limits to welfare assessments placed on general-equilibrium systems.

These matters will be discussed at length in later sections, but it may be helpful to sketch out in advance a line of theoretical argument concerned with the single problem of complexity measurement.

Consider these quotations which are drawn from *The Economy of Cities* by the distinguished urbanist Jane Jacobs.[a]

... McCormick's first horse-drawn reaper was a tremendous innovation for farm work; here was a machine that replaced hand implements and supple, complex hand movements. Although this idea and the device to carry it out were new to farm work, the same idea and devices similar in principle were already commonly used in industrial work. Nor could McCormick have manufactured the reaper if other industrial tools had not already been developed. The industrial revolution occurred first in cities and later in agriculture.

The difference, once a city has grown explosively, is that its local economy contains so many more kinds of exportable goods and services than it did when the city was small and young and its local economy meager. The larger a city's local economy grows, the more it contains that is immediately or potentially exportable ... "Everything's up to date in Kansas City, they've gone about as fur as they kin go," ... First comes news of what people have in this city or that. Then, in time, come some of the things themselves. Others you always have tо go to the city to get.

City—A settlement that consistently generates its economic growth from its own local economy.

Town—A settlement that does not generate its growth from its own local economy and has never done so.

These descriptions form part of an insightful but nevertheless groping attempt to capture the complexity dimension of an active viable city. Regenerative growth is an attribute of the viable city, and such growth is associated with intrinsic complexity: the presence of "critical masses" of specialized workers, "infrastructure bases" of industries, and "threshold levels" of communication systems. These attributes, in turn, require that the city exceed a certain minimum size and that it have passed through a process of development that leaves it with appropriate specialized resources as part of its industrial base. Once we have

---

[a]References mentioned in the text or in the footnotes are to works in the Bibliography.

gone this far, it is natural to ask if these complexity characteristics are at all susceptible to measurement and rigorous definition. It is true that a modern industrial economy is more "complex" than the economy of a primitive tribal system. It is also true that modern industrial economies have become more complex with the passage of time. What, however, does the term *complexity* mean in these contexts? Can we say that complexity is a qualitative state that can be identified unambiguously? Going further, is it possible to attach a measure to complexity so that one can make numerical assessments of the complexity of economic systems and accordingly compare, rank, or predict?

Very little illumination on these matters can be obtained from conventional data sources and analytic methods. For example, an economic system appears to be "more complex" if a greater number of transactions is required to generate a single unit of final production. The presence of such complexity might be inferred from descriptive proxies; i.e., transactions velocity, the number of telephones *per capita*, or the ratio of categories in the Yellow Pages to number of firms. Such indices are suggestive of infrastructural elements, but have no intrinsic explanatory power.

Perhaps one could inspect the structure of a production through an input-output model and associate greater complexity with a greater number of readily identified activities, a greater number of nonzero entries (for a given number of activities), or inability to decompose the system into distinct sectors or blocks. In a parallel example, degrees of complexity might also be suggested by the structure of flow-of-funds tables describing intermediation within the system. In the same spirit, one could examine the basic characteristics of a working econometric model that passes appropriate tests of parsimony, fit, and predictive accuracy, etc. Greater complexity might be indicated by a relatively large number of endogenous variables, a relatively large number of equations, and/or a particularly intricate recursive structure.

In these cases (input-output, flow-of-funds, and econometrics) *complexity* could be given qualitative meaning through analysis of the structural characteristics of the models used to represent the system. One could even go so far as to use, as a measure of complexity, the computer time needed to calculate solutions for the models (or simulations based on the models). However, the operational defects of such approaches to defining complexity are apparent. It is hardly possible to standardize techniques of modeling so as to exclude one model-builder's predisposition toward overelaboration and another's toward misspecification. Rarely, if ever, will it be the case that a feasible sectoralization of a descriptive model will correspond to the functional organization of the system. In this connection note that, despite intuition that tells us that there is a difference, there is no robust way to distinguish a production function estimated for Malta from one estimated for Western Europe by simple inspection (recognizing that the production function concept may be otherwise tainted).

In short, there are very few practical means available to the economist, planner, or behavioral scientist who wishes to examine the complexity dimension. Thus the matter has remained outside the main body of economic theory, although there is a long list of pressing problems in applied fields which await solutions, pragmatic methods, or insights. To establish a context for the analysis embarked on here, a few such problems are presented now:

1. Relationships between social structures and industrial structures are continuing themes in social criticism, industrial psychology, and social psychology. The demands of "complex" organizational and work relationships are often cited, but, lacking a formal concept of "complexity," the analysis remains at a descriptive and nonquantitative level.
2. In development economics, complexity issues enter under the heading "infrastructure requirements and absorbtive capacity"; in urban economics, under the heading "critical levels of specialization"; and in regional economics, under the heading "autarky analysis." The complexity of the system is critical in all these cases.[b]
3. Although not treated formally in pure capital theory, the complexity dimension is obviously a critical factor in technical change. It invariably appears in historical and verbal descriptions of technology; it is invariably neglected in the quantitative development, growth, or production models used to describe it.
4. The complexity dimension has relevance to the emerging policy question of the sensitivity of highly organized systems to disruption. The "energy crisis" and strikes in critical industries or sectors raise doubts as to the resiliency and capacity of the system to adjust. The thought is in the air that organized "efficient" systems may not be resilient in the face of disruptions, but that a "less-efficient" more complex system may be able to regenerate substitutes for lost or disrupted activities.
5. The problem in (4) has an associated planning counterpart: will the loss of a critical industry cause a previously viable unit to degenerate into a ghost town, or will it regenerate a substitute?
6. The problem in (4) and (5) has a counterpart in strategic analysis—what is the core of an economy, and are there sectors which, if destroyed, will lead to system destruction? The selective destruction of components is a subject for simulation which may realize the notion of testing for "compressability."[c]

These are the problems. How can they be approached? The claim is that complexity measurement in an economy composed of congeries of individual

---

[b]One can say that Jane Jacobs' work *The Economy of Cities* is entirely about this subject. Infrastructure is a standard concern of development economists; Kindleberger (Chapters 1, 6, 7) is particularly informative.

[c]Compressibility of an economy is an intuitive notion that recurs in discussions of activity models of large systems. Morgenstern (see Bibliography) has attempted to formalize the concept.

behavioral and productive units is conceptually related to the problem of analyzing the structure of versatile and powerful computers. Von Neumann's approach (oriented to proving the existence of an abstract machine that has the capacity to reproduce itself) is particularly instructive. Von Neumann's model involved the representation of a machine as a constellation of components and functional parts, each described as a particular state assumed by an automaton.

It was shown by von Neumann that a significant system function, such as computational power or self-reproduction, could only be accomplished by a machine that had attained a particular scale threshold and contained more than a particular threshold number of differentiated components. The complexity and richness of the system became critical factors, and, following this focus, subsequent studies developed techniques for analysis of the different aspects of complexity: the field of interaction over which a component operates, the connectivity of such fields, and the intrinsic complexity of the individual component. The approach extends into the comparative analysis of structural complexity in terms of derived measures associated with each of these attributes. It will be shown that this line of analysis can be fruitful in the economic domain as well.

To substantiate this claim, we must show the following: first, that economic units and collections of such units can be represented as automata; second, that the representations themselves are practical, meaningful, credible, and insightful; third, that complexity measures can be calculated for abstract automata models of economic systems and subsystems; fourth, that such calculations are an advance over ordinary qualitative assessments; and fifth, that such calculations are a source of significant theory.[d] In brief, this task entails the development of an automata format for all relevant economic units and behaviors—the problem of *smallest unit representation*—and then the complexity analysis of the structure of the SUR model.

It turns out that numerical complexity measurement is a direct consequence of SUR model structure. A single numerical index of complexity can be calculated, but it turns out to be of greater interest to operate with a small number of complexity parameters which indicate separately the intrinsic complexity of the individual components of the system, the complexity of various chains of interaction, and the effective range of influence of a single component. If desired, the list of computable parameters can be extended to

---

[d]To take a classic example, the claim translates into an assertion that one can, at the very least, take Adam Smith's image of the pinmaking process and produce an explicit comparison between pinmaking as carried out by a single highly skilled artisan and pinmaking as carried out under factory organization with the rationalization and specialization of tasks and subtasks. In the first instance, one would model a highly complex *individual* component (the skilled artisan-merchant); in the second instance, one would model a highly complex *system* of *simple* components (machines and ordinary workers). Measures would be available for both system and component complexity, and these measures would be placed in correspondence with characteristics of physical capital, organizational skills and resources, and available infrastructure.

cover the characteristics of subcomponents and subsystems. Now we come back to the original question of the computer-system: economic-system analogy: it is extremely useful to think of the problem of complexity measurement as akin to the problem of describing an advanced IBM 370 System computer in comparison to simpler versions and also in comparison to predecessor models in the 7000 series or 650 series. The descriptive parameters (core size, number of relays, number of I/O channels, number of satellite computers, core size of a satellite computer) are analogous to those that would be used to describe the system characteristics of an economy. In brief, as the operating characteristics, flexibility, range and versatility of a computing system can be described effectively by established and recognized engineering specifications; analogous descriptive principles appear to apply to the larger socioeconomic system. We now consider the plan and order in which we shall develop these and related conceptions.

Organization and Exposition

This book seeks to present both a method and a body of doctrine. It reverses the usual organization and proceeds from applications to theory on the grounds that readers will be less resistant to theoretical explorations with an unfamiliar method if they have had some experience with the method at an applied level. Following this expositional strategy, Chapter 1 begins with an intuitive description of CA and SUR models, while Chapter 2 outlines actual simulation experience. Chapter 3 offers foundation theory in the CA discipline and applications in economics relating to complexity measurement. Chapter 4 studies applications relating to technical change, while Chapter 5 extends applications to some novel structural conjectures. In Chapter 6 a number of strands are tied together to form a parable of the developmental process. Chapter 7 extends the analysis into the domain of pure welfare theory.

These varied and interlocking connections pose a difficult problem of exposition. The representation of detailed demographic interactions and their relationship to economic processes is of particular interest to one group of economists, while the analysis of capital-using sequences leading to derivation of general-equilibrium conditions appeals to another. The problem stems from the fact that the two groups speak quite different languages and read different literatures in different libraries. The SUR, CA approach calls for some crossover but no special requirements or breadth. There are, after all, many economists who operate von Neumann or Sraffa systems without giving a second thought to the procedures of estimating input-output coefficients. And there are, undoubtedly, many who are expert in such empirical calculations but who are unconcerned with the theoretical properties of abstract systems based on their efforts. We recognize this split but nevertheless wish to give scope to what we believe to be a cooperative interplay between the empirical-simulation aspect and the pure-theory aspect.

Chapters 1 and 2 are focused on the empirical-simulation aspect and interest. They are self-contained and present a simplified but sufficient version of CA theory for operational calculation. Practical considerations involved in developing a computable model are stressed, and actual simulation and rule-building experience is described. Chapters 3 and 4 are oriented to the capital theorist; these chapters are also self-contained, but build on deeper mathematical ideas and toward more fundamental economic relationships. The reader can begin with Chapter 3 and look back to Chapters 1 and 2 simply to confirm that what is asserted to be computable can actually be programmed. The final chapters unite the strands by presenting planning, development, and welfare models with links to both interests. Hopefully they will also suggest empirical possibilities beyond those sketched in Chapters 1 and 2 and confirm the capital-theoretic setting of the model. The book invites skimming and skipping from section to section. In most instances, the chapters are mathematically self-contained, but as an aid to the reader, an appendix to this chapter gives an introduction to some basic automata concepts. The book does not demand mathematics beyond college algebra and some familiarity with mathematical presentations in the social sciences. In terms of mathematical progression, Chapters 1 and 2 require no background beyond some second-hand knowledge of applied simulation. Chapters 3 and 4 are somewhat dense with set-theoretic and logical notations but are self-contained mathematically. Chapter 5 refers to some deep but accessible results in automata theory and logic; even so, the arguments presented are intuitive rather than formal. Chapter 6 is the least mathematical chapter but contains some novel theory. Chapter 7 is the most demanding chapter in terms of its referents in general-equilibrium and welfare theory and its use of formal proof. I have tried to fit notations to the specific requirements of the subject matter in each chapter. This results in shifts from chapter to chapter in style and symbols. Because of this and because of the general unfamiliarity of automata theory, an introductory description of automata concepts is given as an Appendix to the Introduction.

Despite the serious purposes just expressed, it bears mentioning that CA theory has developed coteries both openly and covertly for its aesthetic, metaphysical, and recreational qualities. The underground recreational aspect impinges on us all. Inquire at your computer facility if programs for the "game of Life" exist. The answer will be affirmative. Ask next whether the programs give cathode display output, output on film or on curve plotters (as well as standard printouts). The answer will be affirmative but guarded since the next question, How much time gets wasted here on the game of Life, anyway?, will confirm all your doubts and misgivings as to the inefficiency of the system and your experience with slow turnaround. "Life" is explained briefly in a supplement to Chapter 1. Some experience with "Life" will confirm the aesthetic characteristics. The metaphysical dimensions concern (1) the possibility of representing matter in space as CA phenomenon; (2) the possibility of recapitulating both phylogeny and ontogeny as CA processes.

If no other objectives are served, perhaps this book will introduce the reader to a new pleasure.

Appraisal of the Technique

The previous paragraphs describe an ambitious program, and a few additional comments are needed to give the reader some perspective on how to assess this work.

1. It should be noted that when used for simulations the SUR technique has no particular advantages in representing optimizing, preference, and choice behavior.[e] Simulations can specify rule-of-thumb or lexigraphic choice behavior quite simply, and choices based on simple objective functions or on power indices have also been successfully modeled (see Chapters 1 and 2). However, it is awkward (though hardly impossible) to develop a practical system embodying a wide range of individual preferences, although such preference structures are implicit in theoretical versions.
2. SUR provides no new advantages in modeling markets. Market phenomena can be included in a simulation by deriving data from the main SUR routine, calculating market prices in an external subroutine, using standard econometric formulations, and then reintroducing the new prices as changed boundary conditions. It is awkward (but, again, not impossible) to model the market directly.
3. The greatest advantages of the technique seem to be in explicit representation of physical transactions, social relationships, detailed production structures, and changing structures. Pricing and monetary aspects seem best handled as derived phenomena in simulation, although they can be incorporated in standard fashion within theoretical analyses.

The earlier claims and the qualifications just listed suggest parallels between SUR at its present stage of development and input-output during its earliest applications: use of physical data which were utilized in preceding quantitative analyses, emphasis on explicit system structure and organization, diminished attention to pricing and market aspects. Finally, one notes that in the abstract mode, input-output analysis has considerable power as a technique for theorem-proving in general-equilibrium, planning, and dynamic contexts. A similar claim is made for SUR.

---

[e]M.L. Picolli (1973) has used a special pattern-recognition *CA* variant to study social choice. This line is not covered in the present book.

Appendix to the Introduction: The Automaton Concept

This appendix aims to clarify the concept of "automata" through examination of several automaton models. We begin with a description of the McCullough-Pitts *neuron*, an abstract representation of a primitive biological unit or electronic component. We will examine the combining and logical properties of neurons, particularly as they can be connected to form *neural networks*, and we will touch on correspondences between abstract neural networks and complex systems such as computing machines.

It is a comparatively simple step to proceed from the neural network to the concept of a network as a basic element or building block in a more complicated system. *Cellular automata* can be thought of as individual networks wired to one another in a regular, repeated pattern or array. In later chapters we will develop the cellular automata concept in somewhat different mathematical formats, but the line of thought presented in this appendix is intuitively satisfying and of historical significance in the evolution of automata studies.

The Turing machine is the final automaton concept to be considered at this time. The Turing model is one of the great mathematical conceptions; a foundation element in the theory of mathematical logic, it also provided the logical basis for modern programming and computer design. The Turing machine format has metaeconomic significance but turns out to be unwieldy in explicit modeling applications as compared to cellular-automata formats. However, it is suggestive as to matters in pure welfare economics and is used as a basis for proof in the final chapter of the book.[a]

---

[a]The Turing machine concept is suggestive as to the metaphorical content of economic models. Much of the literature in mathematical economics is concerned with representing socioeconomic systems by finite-state mathematical forms. This convention is standard, yet it bears further inspection. An important element in society is a constantly expanding mass of archives: history, documents, data banks, and the memories of individuals living and dead. The data in the archives at any instant of time is finite, but the manner in which it increases poses special problems. Suppose we rephrase the description of society (and models representing society) to read: "society is formally representable by a finite-state device (the general-equilibrium equations of the system) which connects to an indefinitely expandable collection of archives." If this description is correct, then there may be serious potential errors in treating the system as if it were finite-state. The question of existence of general-equilibrium solutions becomes one of system solvability, and as we will see later in the Appendix and in Chapter 7, prior judgments on solvability are logically untenable. A full investigation of these questions is beyond the scope of the book, so we leave the matter in a conjectural state and hope that the reader is tantalized to pursue the line.

**Automata: The General Concept and
One Primitive Example**

An automaton is essentially a "black box," a device that generates a prescribed type of output, for a prescribed type of input. As such, one can describe automata in a number of different ways. The type of description one picks usually corresponds to the requirements of the problem at hand—highly abstract forms are chosen for theorems applying to the class of automata, restricted special forms are chosen for their resemblance to real-world counterparts and for their combining properties. Let us first consider an example of an abstract form and then move on to some important special varieties and combining types.

An Abstract Tabular Representation

To begin, let us adopt a chronological convention and stipulate a clock that measures discrete intervals of time. All automata that will concern us are synchronized to this clock, and we agree that "inputs" are received at one moment of time and that "outputs" are uniformly emitted a tick of the clock later.

   Given the convention of the clock, the elements of an automaton consist of the list of items that are recognized as inputs, another list of items labeled outputs, and a specification of the ingredients needed to turn inputs into outputs. One general description of an automaton is given here as Notation 1. Other notations will be introduced at appropriate times.

Notation 1. An *automaton* is a five element system or 5-tuple which is designated $\langle X, Y, Z, \delta, \omega \rangle$. Taking each element in turn:

   X *is a finite set of input symbols.* In one instance, the symbols might be the numerals $(0, 1, 2, 3, 4, 5, 6, 7, 8, 9)$; in other instances, X might consist of the binary symbols (0,1), the letters of the alphabet, or a list of words such as (high, medium, low, off).

   Y *is a finite set of output symbols.* Y might be identical to X. For example, numerals might be accepted as inputs and emitted as outputs. On the other hand, Y might be different from X, as in a control automaton which accepts as inputs (high, medium, low, off) and generates outputs (hot, warm, cold).

   Z *is the finite set of internal states* which can be assumed by the automaton. Z can be thought of as the set of all possible configurations for a specific device. The ith internal state $Z_i \in Z$ (read as "Z_i is an element in Z") is a specific configuration. Z^t is the configuration taken by the device at time t. The meaning of this description will become clearer as we consider the operating or transition functions δ and ω along with some examples.

δ *is the next-state function.* It operates to alter the internal state of the automaton from one tick of the clock to the next. Specifically, δ generates an internal state $Z_i \in Z$ according to the internal state of the preceding period Z^{t-1} and the input signal received then, $X^{t-1} \in X$. In the mathematical literature, δ is described as a mapping of $X * Z$ into Z. $X * Z$ is a set which contains as elements all possible combinations of input signals and internal states. δ associates an element in Z with each element in $X * Z$.

ω *is the output function* and consists of a similar mapping of $X * Z$ into Y. In other words, ω gives a unique output signal for each combination of an internal state and input signal.

These definitions are easily illustrated through an example which tabulates the behavior of a simple automaton. Suppose we have as the set of input symbols the words (high, medium, low, off) and as the set of output symbols the words (hot, warm, cold). "Medium" is thus an element in the set X, while "cold" is an element in the set Y. An internal state Z_i determines whether "hot," "cold," or "warm" will be the response to a specific input signal. For example, in Table A-1, Z_1, the first column, generates an output of "hot" regardless of input, while Z_2 gives different responses to different input signals (and appears to behave as some sort of temperature-control system). Z, accordingly, is the set of all possible internal states (read, control positions) that the automaton can assume; an arbitrary and partial list is given in the table. ω is the table itself.

We know from the table that if the automaton is in the internal state Z_1, the function ω determines that an input signal of "high" results in an output of "hot." But this is not the whole story; the input signal in conjunction with the existing internal state may cause the automaton to adjust its internal configuration. This is accomplished through δ which picks for each Z_i and X_i a unique element of Z to operate in the following time period. For example if Z_1 were operating in the initial time period and the signal were "high," a possible next-state function would put the system into Z_2 in the succeeding period but

Table A-1
The Input-Output Behavior of an Automaton—The Function ω

Input Signals	Internal States				
	Z_1	Z_2	Z_3	...	Z_N
High	Hot	Hot	Warm	...	Cold
Medium	Hot	Warm	Warm	...	Warm
Low	Hot	Warm	Cold	...	Warm
Off	Hot	Cold	Cold	...	Hot

Outputs

leave the system in Z_1 if the signal were "off," "medium," or "low." The class of all automata operating in these particular symbols is describable in terms of the permutations formed by the set products, but particular applications may specify an automaton operating on a selection among these permutations. For example, the next-state function might be defined so that it would be impossible to go into Z_1 unless the system were in Z_1 initially.

The abstract formulation fits a great number of mechanical and computational devices and suggests that a fair class of economic models are so describable. In a computer, for example, the entire memory and processing registers are in a particular state Z_i; an input signal (datum) is received, and this causes the internal state of the machine to change and leads to an output being generated. (In many program applications, the output of one period becomes the next period's input.) The computer itself is described by Z, the set of all possible internal states; X, the symbols received as input; and Y, those used in output. δ and ω are given by the hardware.

Many single activities or processes fit the description, but larger-scale, richer forms do as well: an input-output model, for example, processes a set of input commodity symbols (tons of wheat, pounds of rice, kilowatts of electricity, etc.) into a set of output commodity symbols. (A number of other automata associations are given later in Table A-2.) A specific element of Z for such a model is a set of activities (a matrix of production coefficients) and a resource set; the next-state function determines the next period's initial resources (and possible modifications of the activities in a fully dynamic model). The algebra of input-output systems and other related models can be formally explored without reference to the automaton notation and concept; the reason for introducing Notation 1 and the automaton referent in this connection is to show that an automaton basis exists for aggregate economic forms and to prepare the ground for examining primitive automata that combine to form systems analogous to a standard input-output system. We simply note at this time that in the standard input-output model, the next-state and output functions are formed by specific solution algorithms which correspond to the solutions of a set of linear equations. When the problem is placed in the automaton framework and we see the system as a composition of primitive automata, other computable solution methods with economic meaning will emerge. In other words, the matrix-inverse solution is only one element in a larger class of next-state and output functions that may be economically acceptable.

Primitive Automata

A primitive automaton is a device that fits the definition given as Notation 1, but which, because of its simplicity, special characteristics, reasonable restrictions on δ and ω, and resemblance to a real-world referent, has substantial

Table A-2
Automata Associations

Representation	(Signal) Input State	Internal State	Output State (or Next State)	Comments
Addition register	4	3	7	An automaton that is a component of a larger system
Computer regression routine	Data	Stored program-initialized registers	Printout	This is actually one configuration within the class of programs.
Nerve cell	Heat stimulus	{ Sensitive Not sensitive	{ Pain No reaction	A classic automaton the McCullough-Pitts cell (see Minsky)
Neural net	Heat stimulus	Open channel "memory"	Movement to switch on air conditioner	This system is a configuration of simple nerve cells. It can be represented by a single complex-state automaton.

Table A-2 (cont.)

Representation	(Signal) Input State	Internal State	Output State (or Next State)	Comments
Worker (one of a number of conditions that can be assumed by a person)	Presence of tool, Price signal, Wage signal	18 to 65 years old; not otherwise employed, Wealth level	Product level	Output determined by a standard optimization routine (note the aging of the worker and the accumulation of experience are separately accounted for).
Machine on production line	Price signal, Available workers, Available new material	Index of potential production, Age	Product	Optimization calculation (aging and depreciation calculation)
Farmer	Capacity of neighboring plots of land, Available day labor	Workforce status, Working capital	Product, Fertilization of land	Optimization calculation
Agricultural sector	Fertilizer price	Average productivity of available land plots	Product; internal terms of trade	Individual plot fertility levels determined by micro-decisions (farmer)

heuristic power. Our eventual interest will be with cellular automata, primitives that correspond to economic units and have superb aggregating and combining powers, but it will be helpful to begin discussion with one of the simplest primitives, the McCullough-Pitts model of the neuron.

The Neuron Model. Figure A-1*a* gives a pictorial representation of neuron. The arrows leading to the neuron represent two input channels (nerve fibers). Each channel can carry an impulse, i.e., be in an "excited" state, or it can be in a "rest" (or "quiescent") state. The number in the body of the neuron is a "threshold"; if the number of impulses exceeds the threshold, the neuron emits a signal through the output channel (nerve fiber) from it. The neuron pictured in *a* corresponds to an or switch (a signal on either input channel generates an output response). Figure A-1*b* illustrates an "and" switch, while Figure A-1*c* illustrates a "majority" switch. In these cases the input and output signals are simply "off" and "on" (or, are considered as binary data), and the output functions are easily tabulated (clearly the *next-state* function in these cases is trivial).

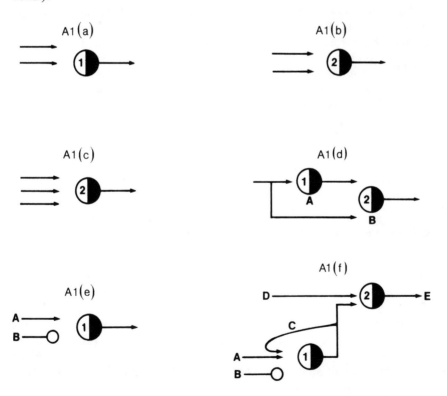

Figure A-1. Neurons and Neuron Nets

Neural Nets. Figure A-1d illustrates a composition of neurons, or a neural net. The neuron labeled A imposes a one-period delay on a signal; thus, the neuron labeled B fires only if there have been two successive impulses down the input channel.[b] Treating the composition of neurons as a single automaton, we see that the system can assume one of two possible internal states—corresponding to whether A is firing—and there is therefore a nontrivial next-state function. (Again, the behavior of this compound automaton can be tabulated according to the definition under Notation 1.)

In Figure A-1e an *inhibitory* input fiber B extends to the neuron as well as an ordinary channel A. An impulse along the inhibitory channel shuts down output so that the logic of this cell is A, and not B. Figure A-1f exhibits a neural net with a "memory." A signal is sent down the channel D; an output registered at E means that at some earlier time an impulse was sent down channel A and no inhibiting input was sent down B. Channel C, a feedback loop, is needed to complete the system. The logic is clear-cut, but obviously this representation abstracts from many real problems of signal attenuation and required amplification, as well as from problems of error-sensing.

Figure A-1 illustrates just a few of the varieties of neural cells and neural nets. Neural automata of these types can be combined in series to form intricate lag response functions; or signals can be split and fed into batteries of neural automata to obtain intricate behaviors. The McCullough-Pitts neuron and neural nets have had and continue to have wide use as models for theoretical investigations of biological systems and artificial intelligence. The model, however, loses its visual appeal and becomes awkward to handle when one comes to examine systems of like elements or components that are wired together in an interactive fashion. The cellular-automaton model provides a format for handling such systems, and, as this book will show, the format extends to cover rich and detailed socioeconomic behaviors.

Cellular Automata

Figure A-2a illustrates a wired-together system of neural nets, which are pictured in a highly abstract format. The object M is a bank of "memory" nets such as the one in Figure A-1f. In effect, M contains digital information that constitutes the internal state of the automaton. C is a bank of "control" nets, such as those in Figure A-1a through e. C receives information along the input channels to the automaton and "writes" on M in accordance with the flow of information and the internal state of M at $t - 1$. The output wires transmit the internal state of

---

[b]This and other neural nets have obvious neurophysiological referents, and the neural-net model is much used in studies of natural and artificial intelligence.

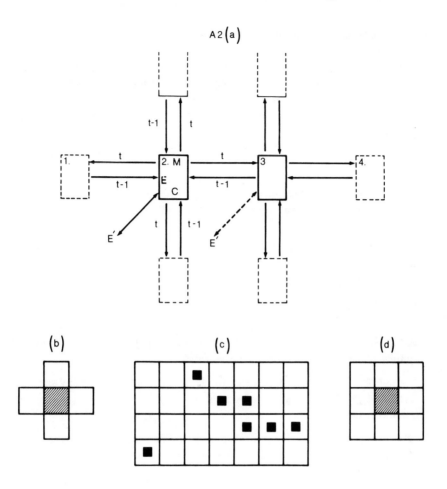

Figure A-2. The Imbedding of a Neuron Net into a Cell.

the automaton. In effect, each automaton is synchronized with the system clock, each broadcasts its internal state at $t-1$, the control calculations are made in the interval from $t-1$ to t, and internal states are altered and rebroadcast at time t. As an added feature, the dotted line leading from E to E' broadcasts the automaton's internal state to an external "monitor" outside the system.[c]

We note that this type of composition of automata is an automaton itself by the preceding definition—all components are automata, and regardless of the complexity of their composition, we have not gone beyond the finite lists of

[c]The return channel suggests that the monitor (whether a live body or another automaton) has the capacity to influence the control from outside the boundary proper.

symbols for input and output and the finite set of states that can be entered in the memory banks (as long as the number of automata in the system is itself finite). This is a very rich system formed out of components that are themselves compositions of primitive elements. The only artificiality in the scheme is the restricted "wiring diagram" which only allows automata to directly influence their near neighbors. For action at a distance, a cell would have to influence intermediate automata, which would pass the influence along with the passing of time.[d]

For obvious reasons, systems of the sort just described are labeled cellular automata, and there are notational and illustrative conventions that add to the convenience of using this format. When we are concerned primarily with heuristic or representational applications, the following nomenclature is convenient.

Notation 2. A cellular-automaton model is a system composed of finite-state automata embedded in a cellular space. The elements in the system are described below.

A *cellular space* is an infinite lattice or grid. Each enclosed grid unit is labeled a *cell.*

A *cellular automaton* is a finite-state automaton as before. Each cell of the cellular space contains a copy of this automaton.

The automaton can be described as an element that can take on any state V_i in a *state set V. V* is finite and contains V_0, which is distinguished as the *quiescent state.*

The *neighborhood* of cell j is a set of cells in fixed orientation to cell j. The neighborhood can be pictured by a *template* or *overlay* that designates the cells in the neighborhood set.

The *transition function* gives the state of cell j at time t as a function of the state of cells in the neighborhood of cell j at time $t - 1$.

A *system* containing the above elements is *finite* if it contains a finite number of automata in a nonquiescent state (a state other than V_0).

For the most part, the nomenclature is self-evident, but it may be useful to relate it to the example given in Figure A-2. The cellular space is a square lattice organized in cells as in the diagram. Each cell contains a copy of the pictured automata. The cell state corresponds to the internal state recorded in the memory banks of the automata, the neighborhood to the wiring pattern, and the rules to the operation of the control in forming the next-state and output functions.

---

[d]In Figure A-2 the automaton labeled 1 could influence the states of automata 2, 3, 4 in 1, 2, 3 periods respectively. Clearly the system could have been wired differently, so that the long-distance influence could occur in less or more time.

The neighborhood template in the pictured case is compact and tight. It is usually labeled the von Neumann neighborhood for its use in that author's work. Another common neighborhood is the "Moore neighborhood" (named for E. Moore, see Figure A-2), but more complicated or extensive templates can also be used. Specific applied cases may make it convenient to draw up complicated templates, as, for example, if one wished to simultaneously model close-in effects (e.g., between adjacent "families" treated as automata) and broader effects (e.g., labor market effects extending to all families in a region). In such instances, it may be good modeling practice to draw up separate templates for each effect and to use a computer in calculating their overlap.

It turns out that the behaviors of an automaton operating in an arbitrary neighborhood set can be *simulated* by a different CA model specifying the von Neumann or Moore template (see Chapter 3). This fact helps in establishing a common basis for cross-model comparisons of complexity and for standard analyses; nevertheless, for applied representations and for empirical work it makes a great deal of sense to operate with "realistic" templates. Lines and areas of influence are generally easy to conceptualize; and, as a form of empirical material, such data are frequently available though seldom utilized.

Noting again that overlapping distinct templates are likely to be used in social science applications, it should be mentioned that "laminar" organization of a CA model is of great potential utility. In a laminar system one models distinct behaviors on distinct cellular spaces; for example, demographic behavior in a cellular space where the automata are people or households, agricultural production in a space labeled "land" and where the automata are farms, industrial production in factory space, and so forth. In such a system, each space is synchronized to the common clock, and each is oriented to a common spatial grid. Templates may be limited to a single lamination, or a cell on one lamination may have a neighborhood on another (as, for example, where "farm" production requires a "workforce" drawn from the "demographic" plane). In a laminar system one can simultaneously have a blend of very intricate microbehaviors (at the level of the household) and rather broad macrobehavior (at the industry level). In this organization one can have the industry portion of the system operating in an approximate general equilibrium, while local equilibria rule on other laminations. In practice, this means that one can build a system which has the disaggregation detail of a 10,000-by-10,000 input-output model but which only requires a systemwide solution for a subsystem perhaps equivalent to a 20-by-20 input-output model. There will, of course, be myriads of local computations and decisions on other laminations, but those are easily calculated. The question of whether this is a meaningful way to compose a system remains.

CA systems can be built with very simple neighborhoods, rule structures, and state spaces (see Box 1 in Chapter 1). But social science applications will tend to call for more elaborate systems. Obviously, one can build extremely complicated systems by using the cellular-automaton format, but one can also specify a variety of "associations" with the individual component cell: a constructing machine, an entire computing system, a sector of an economy providing input to the system being modeled. The cellular automaton is simply described in terms of the cellular space in which it operates, an enumeration of input, internal and output states, and a specification of the neighborhood(s) over which interactions occur. This description, as we will see, allows specification of a wide range of economic and sociological phenomena. In using the general mathematical description, one can drop the wired-in circuitry associations and proceed as did von Neumann with the broadest behavioral and system referents.

The broad notation can be given now. In this version we allow the cellular space to be multidimensional (d-dimensional) and enter a time utilization factor, T, which indicates how efficiently this particular automaton might be simulated by a reference automaton (say, one with the von Neumann neighborhood). Otherwise the elements are familiar and entirely consonant with those given earlier.

Notation 3. A cellular-automaton model is described by the characteristics $\langle Z^d, f, V_0, V, S, N, T \rangle$. These are exhibited in the following statements:

Z^d is a d-dimensional integer lattice (or d-dimensional vector space)

Z_i is a cellular space with automaton components

f_i is the transition function for Z_i

V_{0i} is the quiescent state

V_i is the state set and S_1 the state index

N is the neighborhood index for the d-D neighborhood template N_i of cell p; or neighborhood set, N_i, defined

$$[c_r \mid r = p + c_j; \; c_j \in N_i]$$

T_i is a comparison measure for computation time

Notation 3 does contain some new elements, *indices* applying to the neighborhood set, the state set, and to "computation time." These indices are parameters which are descriptive of the complexity and structure of the automaton model. In Chapter 3 we will examine ways in which inferences as to the intrinsic complexity of the real-world referent can be drawn from analysis of the model indices. We note at the moment that such analysis can involve comparisons based on the speed with which different models can calculate transitions for specific reference configurations. The index T_i is a general expression for such comparative measures. The additional notations needed to explore this concept—and to complete Notation 3—will be introduced at the appropriate time. Meanwhile we turn to a review of the materials introduced thus far.

To conclude this section, we again note the generality of the automaton concept—see Table A-2 for automaton referents. We also stress the applicability of the concept in computer science, engineering, life science, and linguistic fields. It follows from earlier descriptions that the symbol constituents of a language, its grammar and its logic are representable by cellular automata. And, accordingly, cellular automata are used in pure linguistic theory. This line of thought is not followed in these notes but references in Minsky and Piccoli (see Bibliography) provide useful introductions to the literature. Piccoli, in particular, follows this line of automaton analysis to develop representations of private- and social-choice mechanisms. Purely mathematical results in group theory and finite semigroups are not developed here, but we should note that automaton formulations in abstract logic do pertain to broad welfare assessments, and so we turn to the concept of the Turing machine.

The Turing Machine

The *Turing machine* is an abstract representation which consists of the following elements: a reading-writing control device, a tape, and a tape factory. Figure A-3 pictures the organization of these components. The control device is a finite-state automaton which corresponds in contemporary language to the hardware of a computer and its operating logic. Among other functions, the control governs backspacing and advance of the tape so that a specific field of the tape can be brought under the input-output head of the device. A tape field can be blank, or it can contain a symbol from a finite list of symbols. The machine "reads" the symbol and responds by altering its internal state. In its new state the machine causes new tape movements or the writing of a symbol on the field or a halt.

Consider a Turing machine which reads a tape on which is initially written

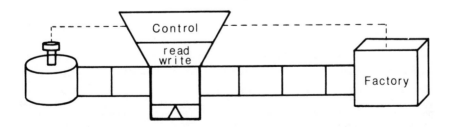

Figure A-3. A Turing Machine

two numbers, for example, (47,5). The control is set to do the following: (1) Read the first number. (2) Advance the tape to the last number written and read it. (3) Compute the number of field advances (in this case, 1). (4) Multiply the number of field advance times the last number read. (5) Advance the tape and write this number. (6) Backspace and compare the number written to the first number. (7) Continue advancing the tape to the last number written, augmenting (step 4) and writing (step 5) until a number is written that exceeds the first number. (8) When this occurs, write the number of field advances and halt.

The problem is effectively solvable; that is, it could be set up by a novice programmer with little difficulty, and there is no ambiguity as to the outcome. Either the machine will halt (as it will with the two numbers given), or it will continue until the tape factory breaks down (as would occur if the second number were negative).

Scratch space may be needed, or conceivably the program writes a lot (e.g., a program that carries out the decimal expansion of π). The tape factory handles the problem-determined needs for tape, and we note in passing that the convention of the tape factory puts mundane resource and economic bounds on the concept of the infinite.

It has been shown and we state without proof the following.[e]

1. Any process which can be naturally characterized as an "effective procedure" can be realized by a Turing machine. This assertion (which in various forms is labeled Turing's thesis or Church's thesis) is not provable since the term "naturally characterized" is intentionally imprecise. The thesis is meaningful in the sense that every procedure which has been proposed by mathematicians as computable or effective in an intuitive sense can be made equivalent to a procedure that can be carried out on a Turing machine.
2. A Turing machine can be shown to be equivalent to more literal models of a computer. This correspondence allows one to consider computability or solvability as an abstract property with significant bridges to realizable concrete procedures.
3. A general Turing machine can be shown equivalent to a Turing machine operating on a two-symbol (binary) language or to a two-state control device operating on a multisymbol language. These equivalences allow a choice of formats for mathematical proof.
4. A Turing machine can realize any computation possible on a finite-state, finite-dimension device. This follows from the specification of the control of

---

[e]These are standard results, which appear in a number of computer science and automata-theory texts. M. Minsky's *Computation, Finite and Infinite Machines* presents these and other findings in an accessible and intuitive way. The relationship between cellular automata and Turing machines is explored in various pieces by A.R. Smith (see the Bibliography and discussions in Chapter 3).

the machine as a finite-state device. The converse is not true—this can be shown for any programmable calculation that can overrun a bounded scratch space.

5. A cellular space (e.g., a cellular automaton embedded in an infinite lattice) can simulate a Turing machine (of the most general type). The control device of the Turing machine becomes a finite initial configuration of nonquiescent states in the cellular space. By construction it can be shown that a suitably specified automaton and initial configuration are capable of activating quiescent cells and building "communication channels" out into the lattice where it can develop scratch spaces equivalent to the Turing machine tape.

Comment. The assertions (1) to (4) of the previous paragraph are suggestive of the flexibility and applicability of the Turing machine concept. Assertion (5) is more immediate and of greater importance. For the most part, this text will treat the cellular-automaton framework as a means for analyzing structural relationships within finite-state bounded models of the socioeconomic system (ultimately, a model in which each decision unit and each significant artifact are representable). In their more primitive forms, such models specify simple mechanical rules for state transitions, so that model histories are equivalent to a sequence of internal states and output states in an ordinary computer run. Suppose, however, we specify that some decision units possess computing capacity and the ability to make decisions based on model history and projections from that history. This clearly takes us beyond the primitive bounded CA model and into the domain of the Turing machine. What does this mean? To preview later arguments, we will assert the following. First, analysis of the *structure* of a bounded cellular space at a particular moment of time is entirely unaffected by this concern. It is proper and appropriate to take a model of the socioeconomic system and investigate its complexity in terms of numbers of states, intricacy of interactions, and depth of hierarchy. Similarly, it is reasonable to follow up a *particular* model history. These two applications, complexity measurement and representative simulation (treated respectively in Parts II and I of the book), are unaffected by the epistemological issues raised by the Turing machine metaphor. The problems arise where one attempts to make prior judgments as to system outcomes—as in general-equilibrium theory, where one is concerned with the solvability of the system and the properties of solution, or in pure welfare economics where one is concerned with the correspondence of outcomes to objectives. We will see that there are some unusual solvability problems involved here, problems so significant that a number of standard results are brought into question. Before going on, it should be stressed that this is not a straw-man argument which is raised because of the artificiality of the CA model. Rather the CA description is completely general and subsumes all standard models.[f] The distinction between bounded and unbounded models is not significant in most applications which involve descriptive analyses or tracking of particular dynamic processes; it is absolutely critical where one takes an overall view on system performance. To show this, we carry the Turing machine metaphor one step further and consider the concept of computation universality.

Computation Universality

It has been shown that a Turing machine that exceeds a minimum level of complexity (in terms of the number of internal machine states and the number of symbols in the tape language) can achieve computation universality.[g] The concept is best developed through an example. Suppose we are given a Turing machine T and an input tape τ. T accepts τ, and according to the nature of the problem, either will complete calculations and *Halt* or it will not. A universal computer U will accept as input a tape containing $d(T)$, a description of T, and will replicate the performance of T. That is, given the input tape τ, it will halt where T does and otherwise produce identical output.

The Halting Problem

We now ask if it is possible to build a machine which has the ability to determine whether T will halt with arbitrary input τ. It is clear that the problem is solvable for some input tapes; to show that it is not solvable for all tapes, we simply have to show one contrary case. This can be done rather neatly. Let us suppose we have such a machine. We label it D and load it with input $d(T)$ and τ. If T halts for input τ, D will compute a "yes" and halt. If T does not halt for input τ, D will compute a "no" and halt. For our test case, we use as the tape input $d(T)$ instead of any tape τ. [There is nothing remarkable in this; $d(T)$ will be accepted by the machine as a string of symbols.]

We now construct a machine E which is identical to D except that it contains a few more states which give E the ability to copy tapes. Thus we can feed E a

[f]The standard models involve some aggregation over collections of individual units which can each be described in terms of a finite number of states. Behavioral functions involve the reactions of individuals, units, or valid collections of units to variables such as prices or expected prices, which in turn depend on behavioral functions over the same or different collections. This description applies equally to the Arrow-Debreu model or to a highly aggregated macromodel. There is no difficulty with a cross-sectional analysis of the structure of such a representation nor with a dynamic sequence from particular inherent conditions. These are bounded finite problems. Judgments over the general solvability of such systems are at issue.

[g]See Minsky, Chapters 7 and 8. His notation is followed in what follows. A variant proof appears in Chapter 7 of this book.

tape containing just $d(T)$. It will copy the tape and then proceed to operate just as D would. Thus if D would solve the halting problem, E would also. That is, either E would halt after computing a "yes" if T halts with input $d(T)$, or E would halt after computing a "no" if T does not halt with input $d(T)$.

Now we go one step further in construction and prepare a machine E^* which is identical to E but which contains an additional circuit so that instead of halting after computing a "yes," the machine goes into a permanent loop. Thus far we have that E^* with input $d(T)$ does not halt if T with input $d(T)$ does halt, or

E^* with input $d(T)$ halts, if T with input $d(T)$ does not halt.

Suppose now that we start E^* on a tape which contains a description of itself, that is, $d(E^*)$. From the preceding arguments we have

E^* applied to $d(E^*)$ halts if E^* applied to $d(E^*)$ does not halt.

and

E^* applied to $d(E^*)$ does not halt if E^* applied to $d(E^*)$ halts.

This is an obvious contradiction; tracing back to find reasons for it, we are forced back to the original assertion that D was a possible construction. There is, after all, no difficulty with the construction of E^* given E. This simply involves substituting a subprogram which loops indefinitely for an exit routine. The purpose of the substitution is, of course, to obtain a basis for detecting the contradiction. Similarly, there is no problem with constructing E from D; this simply involves adding a subroutine to D which copies a tape field as the original tape field is brought under the read head. (In fact, one does not even have problems with the infinite here.) The purpose of this step is to obtain comparability with the original condition of simulating T given τ. In short, we are forced to conclude that the machine D is an impossible construction. (Prior constructions T and U have been demonstrated correct although proofs are not given here.)

Lest it be thought that the proof given here is unduly restrictive and limited to the input of the specific tapes $d(T)$ or $d(E^*)$, consider the following argument. A tape is simply a string of symbols: any input tape could contain $d(T)$ or $d(E^*)$ as an embedded string, and there can easily be equivalences between an arbitrary tape τ and those which force the contradiction. A program which could detect such tapes would contradict the proof and would therefore be impossible itself. It should be noted that the proof does not negate the possibility of a machine D^* which can monitor members of a prior restricted class of tapes and problems, but the argument has considerable significance in practical applications. The construction of general debuggers and monitors is in fact a fantasy, and modern computers can only work toward fair approximation of such systems.

Now what does this argument tell us about economic systems and problems of evaluation and analysis? If we assert that an economy can be put into correspondence with a Turing machine and this assertion turns out to be correct, it follows that there is a class of problems concerning the functioning of the system that cannot be answered definitely. The questions, then, are (1) Is the correspondence correct? and (2) What are the unsolvable prior evaluations? We consider each in turn.

The Turing Machine Correspondence

The equivalence between a computation-universal Turing machine and a computation-universal cellular space is well established. The problem of showing the correspondence between such a cellular space and the real world (or an acceptable surrogate model) is quite another matter, and involves appealing to intuition, historical consequences, or empirical sense rather than proof.[h]

The text presents the case for selecting CA constructions in a large number of applications. We simply note that the intuitive bridge to considering models which augment their own state spaces—i.e., rely on their own model histories or extrapolated expectations or internally computed behaviors or recursive conjectures—is facilitated when the structure of the system is first laid out in CA form. The argument here is that one has a tool with which one can identify and describe every decision node in the system (given that one will surely simplify and aggregate in specific applications). Once this potential specification is laid out, it becomes a natural step to investigate the decision criteria of each node. If one or more such decision points are involved as in standard microeconomic optimization, the system as a whole takes on the characteristics of the Turing machine rather than those of a finite automaton.

Unsolvability in Economic Systems

If one accepts the Turing machine correspondence, it follows that certain classes of problems become unsolvable for the system. It is natural to ask if these problems are at all important or interesting. It will take analyses that go beyond the scope of this book to do real justice to the question.

The one example which is developed at length here (in Chapter 7) suggests

---

[h]It is generally accepted that the conditions of individuals, aggregates, and artifacts in the system are describable in terms of a finite number of states. The finite CA model and any number of standard general-equilibrium or dynamic models are consistent with the description. As far as finite, bounded models are concerned, the selection of one model type over another is a matter of taste, need, and style in analysis.

that conditions roughly analogous to "halting" problems restrict the ability to draw conclusions in welfare theory and general-equilibrium analysis, and these restrictions seem to be more inhibiting than those which are standard in the analysis. The halting problem applies in instances in which one wishes to form a prior judgment as to whether system operation will result in compatibility with stipulated objectives (e.g., whether a market process will result in stable equilibria consistent with Pareto optimality, whether a political system will satisfy prior axioms, whether a planning protocol will result in convergence to targets, and so on). If we stipulate that an "evaluative machine" or "welfare economist" will halt calculations when it is discovered that such compatibility exists or that it cannot exist, we are directly in the regime of Turing machine unsolvability. Conjectures in this area are not pursued beyond the theorem given in Chapter 7. A full reevaluation of welfare propositions is well beyond the scope of this book, which, after all, is primarily concerned with structural matters and simulation possibilities which are in no way inhibited by such problems of unsolvability.

Part I:
Smallest Unit Representation

Introduction to Part I

The usual order of exposition in presenting modeling techniques is to proceed from general theoretical and mathematical properties to specific applications. However, in detailing socioeconomic applications of automata methodology, it seems necessary to depart from this convention. Simulation and representation are considered first, in order to reveal the scope and generality of the automaton approach. We will review programming potentialities and simulation experience to point out to the reader the following:

1. The *feasibility* of representation at the level of individual microunits.
2. Modeling *flexibility* which can come from using automata reasoning.
3. The *generality* of the approach in that a general automaton approach can be consistent with the use of standard programming and heuristic models. In fact, such applications are subsumed in the approach.
4. The *cogency* of automaton reasoning in that the standard descriptions of the elements of a socioeconomic system are, in fact, descriptions of automata, so that it is entirely appropriate to theorize in explicit automaton forms. For reasons of expediency in solving problems as well as for historical reasons, conventional modes of analysis have tended to ignore the automaton basis. (This is not necessarily a fault; significant understandings, analytical simplifications, and important results flow from uses of equilibrium reasoning that abstract from structural concerns.)

The argument here is that by virtue of items (1) through (3), one can make practical use of the automaton concept and by (4) warrant such use at a very basic level. These points must be initially established to the reader's satisfaction before the introduction of the theoretical implications of an automaton approach to structure and organization. There are important matters involved here. The text comes back to them repeatedly in later chapters, but the concluding comments in Chapter 1 sketch out some of the main issues.

Finally, in passing, it should also be noted that readers interested primarily in simulation applications will find that Part I provides a sufficient basis for initiating practical applied work.

1

The Logic of Smallest Unit Representation

This chapter gives an initial description of CA theory. The intent is to describe enough of the method to provide a basis for the applied or *representational* approach, where the focus is on model-building and programming. Our concern now is only on showing how to go about developing representations of complex systems and various types of economic and social behavior. In terms of the work as a whole, we will be playing through an exercise. At this time, we will proceed in ad hoc fashion, illustrating potentialities and piling rule on rule as might be done in an applied analysis where the objective is to cover a particular body of data and to include a particular set of relationships. We will place no restrictions on how the programming is to be accomplished and will place minimal restrictions on the logic of the representational model.

The outcome of the exercise will be a computer program. With luck, the program will run and will capture the behavior which motivated the effort. What we will argue at a later point (beginning in Chapter 3) is that the program which is produced as a representational exercise (or as a serious attempt at simulation) may have significance in a larger analysis of the system it portrays. That is, the computer program will be a cellular-automaton model that can itself be simulated by a cellular automaton of a standard or "reference" type. Theoretical analysis of the "simulating" system will provide information about the structural characteristics of the base system—and inferentially about the real world it represents. This information covers the intrinsic complexity of the system and would not be obtainable by other standard means. Furthermore, analysis of the *class* of simulating automata could provide significant capital-theoretic information for the relevant class of economies.

These points could be phrased somewhat differently. This chapter and Chapter 2 provide guidelines to the applied economist or behavioral scientist as to how to construct a particular type of model which will handle relationships and interactions that are hard to capture by other means.

An Outline of the SUR Technique

Our starting point is a set of definitions.

Definitions. A cellular space can be visualized as an infinite "Go" board, checkerboard, or lattice. Each square of the board, a *cell*, is the locus of an

35

individual *automaton*, and each automaton can take on one of a number of prespecified *states* during a discrete time interval. The state of cell j at time t (which corresponds to the state of its embedded automaton) is given by a *transition function* whose arguments are the states of cells in a predefined *neighborhood* of the cell at time $t - 1$. *Time is synchronous for all cells, and the transition calculations are made during the interval between points of time.*

If, for example, the cellular space represents population space, the automaton represents people,[a] and two cell states "live" and "quiescent" are defined, then a snapshot of the cellular space at a moment of time would show the population currently alive. The transition function would determine which cells survive into the next period, which die, and which new cells are born.

Transition calculations can be quite elaborate, but they must be made in an ordered and hierarchic fashion across functions and cells. For example, the transition function could be broken down into three hierarchic subfunctions: a broad "regional" function with a neighborhood consisting of the band of cells three deep around a reference cell, an "immediate locale" function with a neighborhood consisting of the immediately adjacent cells, and an "own" function where the neighborhood is the cell itself. The transition function could then be made up of logical statements such as "*If* cell j is in the live state ("own" function) *and if* there are two live cells in the immediate neighborhood *and if* there are no more than fifteen live cells in the region (*or if* . . .), *then* cell j will remain in the live state." A computer could proceed from cell to cell, calculate according to the programmed logic applied to existing cell states, and then calculate the next cell state.

In an operating model, the individual cell will take on a number of states, corresponding to such demographic and economic characteristics as age, labor force status, educational status, membership in associations, caste, economic income group, social class, and others. Certain characteristics will be determined by the "own" function, e.g., the age state of an individual cell (which depends upon the cell's age state in the preceding period). Other characteristics will be determined at the "immediate locale" level; a birth at cell ij, for example, would require that at least two reproductive adults be present in the immediate locale, while educational status of a cell would depend upon the presence of "educated" cells within the immediate locale during the formative childhood and youth years. Finally, production levels for the system and economic- and social-class levels for the individual cell could depend upon cell states within the wider "region."

In a computerized representation of a socioeconomic system, the computer would, in effect, move from cell to cell in the domain of the program and calculate the cell-state transitions corresponding to "own," "immediate locale," and "regional" effects. the program could then proceed to calculate summary

---

[a]A recreational example of a CA system is presented in Box 1. Practice with the game of Life gives insights into the rich varieties of behavior which can be modeled in SUR research.

statistics over the domain; for example, a census could be taken which gives distributions over any of the demographic characteristics. Production and income aggregates could also be calculated in a more developed system. In effect, "production" of an individual cell is given by its labor force status, by the enumeration of cooperating workers within the region, and by the presence of capital or land within the domain. The land and capital could be given to the system as boundary conditions or, as we will see, as the consequence of separate but interlocking automata processes that are internal to a larger system.

A run of summary statistics form what amount to economic time series for a hypothetical model history. Such data are only one possible output of an SUR program. Other outputs are econometric analyses of the time series, cross-sectional analyses of the economic or social variables for a sample of cells at a point of time, descriptive statistics on the frequency of intercell transactions and interactions, maps of the state space for locational analyses, and measures of the structural stability and effective complexity of the operating system. In practice, all these outputs are produced simultaneously, although, naturally, interest is likely to be focused on only a few of the potentialities at any given time.

Comments. Now, what is the point of this elaboration? Let us suppose for the moment that the time series, summary demographic, and economic statistics are the analytical outputs of immediate interest. How does this output differ from the comparable output of a conventional heuristic study (e.g., one employing industrial dynamics) or from pure analytical results (e.g., variable time paths and side conditions deriving from a two-sector, differential equation growth model)? The answers to this question will illuminate the rationale and singular quality of the SUR approach.

The standard heuristic and analytical models calculate a single time path (for a particular model replication) in variables that summarize microcharacteristics. These models employ a single function (or set of simultaneous functions) over these summary variables. In practice, disaggregation to get at close detail requires total model reconstruction; and, frequently, results at different levels of aggregation will be incompatible with one another.

By contrast, the SUR approach operates from the beginning at an ultimate level of disaggregation, and in practice each microunit computes its own history, taking into account all possible lines of interaction with all other microunits in the system. From a behavioral point of view, any unit capable of choice or independent action is allowed to represent itself, and interactions extend to each plot of land and machine that is also given automata representation. It also turns out that one can effect shifts in the level of aggregation in a single and direct way. A detailed model of "family" behavior at the level of a "village" can be made into a component of a "regional" model which treats the village as the basic unit. One can operate separately at the "village" level, separately at the "regional" level, or at all levels simultaneously.

The problem now is to consider practicalities: What behaviors can in fact be handled meaningfully by SUR? What economic costs and skill requirements are involved in using the approach? And finally, what assurances does one have that SUR is not another ad hoc heuristic fantasy, another *Garbage in/Garbage out* system, except that here the garbage is wrapped in smaller packages?

Theory based on SUR or on the underlying CA theory uses novel—one might even say "far out"—constructs. An economist would be foolish to accept results derived in a new theoretical setting or assertions as to the applicability of that setting without some evidence of potential payoffs of using the scheme in applied analysis. Clearly, activity analysis is now an important abstract setting for theorem-proving; however, many economists would have reservations as to theorems derived in activity-analysis formats, were there not already an impressive list of applications (linear programming, input-output analysis, dynamic programming, etc.) that demonstrate practical benefits which outweigh the burdens of a restrictive linear assumption structure. Accordingly, we now look at the operational qualities of the CA style of modeling.

Formulation of Rules. In developing serious CA versions for behavioral research, it should be recognized first that one can utilize the state space to accommodate a rich fund of demographic, labor force, and behavioral characteristics. For example, designate the basic cellular element H^t as a "household" or "extended family" and associate the state of the cell with the distribution of family members in the demographic categories h_i^t: for example, h_1^t (dependent child), h_2^t (teenager), h_3^t (reproductive-aged worker), h_4^t (post-reproductive worker), h_5^t (aged dependent). The cell state could then be indicated by a 5-byte number, for example, $H^t = (3/4/5/3/2)$, and state transitions could be handled by simple aging rules:

(R_1)   *Rule 1:* Everyone ages one category.

(R_2)   *Rule 2:* Each reproductive adult in H^t produces one offspring in H^{t+1} [e.g., by successive application of R_1 and R_2, $H^t = (3/4/5/3/2) \rightarrow (0/3/4/5/3) \rightarrow (5/3/4/5/3) = H^t + 1$].

Neighborhood Demographic Interactions. In R_1 and R_2 the "neighborhood" of the ith cell is the cell itself, and the rules are conventional "aging" functions with similar associations in other simulation studies. The analysis becomes more interesting where the neighborhood is extended, and the "household" is a "subdivision" placed within a "block" (say the eight orthogonally and diagonally adjacent cells) or a "street" (the subdivision block plus the blocks to the north or south of it). The system detailed here is both eclectic and eccentric in presenting a set of rules that blends characteristics of a tribal society and an urban slum neighborhood. This fantasy construction is intentional and is designed to point out that the actual rule structure can be pure theory (in the pejorative sense) while the individual rules can be quite mundane in character. The reader will note that the parameters of each rule can easily be put into correspondence with empirical data and observations, and that rule structures can be equally realistic. The freedom of controlling parameters and rule structures implies great freedom and range in policy simulation and in pursuit of utopian conjectures. In the policy mode, one can manipulate rules on land fertility in order to judge impacts on social relationships of new agricultural technology, or one can impose a new rule structure (corresponding, say, to forced drafts of workers) on a preexisting technology to assess economic impacts. In the utopian mode, one can in principle indulge such conjectures as tribal or communal social organization coexisting with advanced industrial development.

Rules can express a variety of societal or demographic interactions. For example, the birthrate can respond to neighborhood population density:

(R_3) *Rule 3:* The number of "births" is the rounded integer equal to the number given by R_2 times a "congestion index," say the ratio of block population to predetermined potential population.

Or deaths can result from overcrowding:

(R_4) *Rule 4:* The number of aged dependents is equal to zero if the congestion index exceeds a preset parameter.

Or additional and fanciful social states can be defined:

(R_5) *Rule 5:* A teenager becomes "antisocial" if there are more than m teenagers in the street. In this instance, the original state space must be redefined to include the antisocial state and its complement. (h_2 becomes a double, giving the distribution between antisocial and "socially responsible" teenagers.)

Sociological states can determine economic action:

(R_6) *Rule 6:* Antisocial teenagers have diminished "productivity" in economic activities. (In effect, a production relationship will be defined in which antisocial teenagers produce less output per worker than do others.)

Sociological states can have societal consequences:

(R_7) *Rule 7:* An association labeled a "youth gang" forms if the number of "antisocial teenagers" in a given block exceeds a preset threshold.

Such associations can in turn influence behavior of the basic family unit:

(R_8) *Rule 8:* A family moves to another street if:

Rule 8a: youth gangs form on its block and if:

Rule 8b: there is a "vacancy" (a null cell) within its neighborhood of search (say, two streets to the East and West) and if:

Rule 8c: the "rent" for the vacant apartment is less than 20 percent of the family income ("rent" and "family income" are system-derived magnitudes to be discussed subsequently) and if:

Rule 8d: the family has not moved in the past ten time periods (the state space can be further augmented to include the past migratory history of the unit).

These examples are intended to give a rough idea of the types of demographic and sociological phenomena that can be included with a representation.[b] The programming of such a system is relatively simple; the computer moves from cell to cell calculating transitions for the full set of rules. The program and rule logic can be made to approximate the description of social and economic interactions as they might be given by an ethnographer, an institutional economist, or another skilled observer. The programming itself is comparatively foolproof once one understands a few tricks and conventions for this particular style of work. As we will see, the social relationships and interactions represented in such schemes stand up as subject matter and data for both positive analysis and policy simulation.

It should be clear from these examples that an extraordinary variety of individual situations can arise since an enormous state space could be implicit in a given model. This can be both an analytical advantage and a danger. On the one hand, realistic portrayals are possible; on the other, a glut of incoherent data could be the outcome of overly enthusiastic modeling. Later sections will deal with this class of problem.

Economic Processes

Let us leave the matter of demographic and sociological modeling for the moment and pass on to the modeling of economic processes. We begin with the notion of a laminar cellular space.

Definition: Envisage a cellular space parallel to the original population space (e.g., "laminated *Go* boards"). The new space is labeled "capital," and cells in

---

[b]Schelling has experimented with a similar behavioral model. See the following chapter for a brief discussion of his analysis.

the space can take on m' live states as well as the quiescent state. (The index m' corresponds to an age or vintage of capital.) The "production neighborhood" of c_{kj}, the jth cell in the capital (k) space, is a simple neighborhood of c_{pj}, the jth cell in the population (p) space. Designating neighborhoods by upper-case letters, c_{kj} assumes state m at time t, *iff* C_{pj} contains more than L live cells at time $t-1$. In effect, a cluster of L cells is capable of producing an "economic surplus" realizable as a unit of capital. Additional rules are required to govern the accumulation of capital within c_{kj}, its contribution to production, aging, and eventual retirement. (See Figure 1B-1 for a crude example of this construction.)

In different connections, laminations could represent land, "tool space," "lathe space," "machine space," "factory space," or "final-product space." But let us first consider the simplest illustration, the modeling of an agricultural economy. Let the basic demographic unit be the extended family (as before), but let us drop the urban "block" associations and instead consider the family to be an extended family or peasant household. We now label a second lamination oriented to the demographic plane as "land." Subdivide each land unit into four plots and label the state of a plot as "potential yield" when farmed with m workers. A particular agricultural technology would be represented by a structure of rules similar to those that follow.[c] These rules are presented in intuitive form rather than as the integer state functions which would be employed in practice:

Rule A_1: Cultivation in $t = 0$ results in a reduction of potential plot yield in $t = 1$ (e.g., the state index of plot j is decremented, if it was in the state designated "cultivation" in the preceding period).

Rule A_2: Plot yield can be restored to the maximum by fallowing the land—a reverse aging function applies.

Rule A_3: Plot yield can be restored by increments of fertilizer (e.g., plowing back crops).

Rule A_4: If the land fertility is allowed to decrement below a minimum level, the plot becomes "wasteland" (an unfertile state).

Rule A_5: If a plot touches two other waste plots, it becomes wasteland.

These rules must be triggered by conditions on the demographic plane. Some possible driving conditions are as follows:

Rule A_{6a}: The number of workers in the productive categories of household i are released to work in plots assigned to household i.

---

[c]Many of these rules were devised by M. Katz for a model discussed in the following chapter.

or

Rule A$_{6b}$: The ith household possesses an interpersonal utility function which allows it to optimize the cultivation, fertilization, and fallowing of its corresponding plots. Since the argument of the function is the current demographic and agricultural neighborhood state space, this remains a proper (and computable) transition function.

and

Rule A$_{7a}$: The unit is free to join with neighboring units to pool labor over all or part of joint holdings.

and/or

Rule A$_{7b}$: The unit is free to split off members or move as a unit to occupy land within a predefined land area.

and

Rule A$_{8a}$: Movements splits and labor sharing may be constrained by past cell histories (e.g., transactions between cells originating in the same zone of the space are taboo).

or

Rule A$_{8b}$: Movements splits, labor sharing, etc., may be facilitated by relative power (an index function of the unit's composition and the fertility of land associated with it).

A set of rules such as these can be developed out of empirical data on agricultural technology and from ethnographic information on interactions which are significant in the reference culture. Using such information and the basic laminar model structure, one can represent socioeconomic systems ranging from a slash-and-burn tribal economy to a settled peasant economy. (See Chapter 2 for details.)

Structures such as these are of obvious interest to economic anthropologists and to ethnographers; for present purposes we need only note a few additional characteristics of the model type. First, the production technology in conjunction with the family work force allocation determines the agricultural output for the family unit; this can be taken directly as the measure of "family income." Further distributional rules can be added to the system to correspond to "sharecropping" payments, tax assessments (for policy simulations), interfamily contractual obligations, exploitive payments in respect to "power," etc. In this model type, "family income" serves as the basis for cultivation-optimization decisions *or* can be used in conjunction with a subsistence-consumption requirement to determine deaths from "famine" within the household and the possible generation of "surplus" to finance agricultural development or capital investment.

Industrialization

Of greatest potential interest to economists is the use of SUR to represent advanced capital-using systems. The variety of model subtypes is great: a few are given an outline description below. It should be stressed that a production subtype can be separately programmed and then either examined separately for capital-theoretic information or superimposed over a demographic/sociological submodel.

Subtype 1: Primitive Economy—Simple Tools. Tools are represented as cell states in a lamination oriented to the demographic (and land) planes, while final product is represented by cell states in a separate lamination oriented both to the population work force plane and to the tool plane.

The state of a cell in "tool space" is defined as "periods of productive use remaining," and the following rules generate and age tools.

Rule T_1: The age index decreases one unit with time.

Rule T_2: The age index decreases one unit with use.

and either:

Rule T_{3a}: A "new tool" is purchased or made with S units of "agricultural surplus" (e.g., the index of a cell in a tool space can be incremented if the demographic-agricultural subspace oriented to the tool cell produces a surplus).

or

Rule T_{3b}: Tools are supplied from outside the system according to some (here undefined) regime of "lending" or colonial administration.

The state of a cell in production space is then determined by states in the appropriately aligned joint neighborhood in demographic and tool space. The production rule governing states of cells in a higher lamination corresponds to a production function:

Rule P_{1a}: The product state (number of units produced) is equal to the rounded integer given by λL, where L is the number of free workers in the demographic neighborhood and λ is a parameter empirically determined from outside information.

or

Rule P_{1b}: The product state is given by the rounded-integer solution of any regular neoclassical production function.

or

Rule P_{1c}: The product state is given by an integer, rectangular, production function operating over L and T (as defined before). The production coefficients correspond to handbook data on tool capacity.

The programming of an actual "representation" turns out to be a straightforward process. Heterogeneous capital is represented in a scheme similar to that illustrated in Figure 1-1. Each of the boxes represents a cellular configuration on a specific lamination. The indices (m_i, m_i') designate vintage or other characteristics of the machine. The (s_i, s_i') are the count of machines of a particular type within a designated neighborhood. Certain transition rules correspond to production functions; for example, in sequence S^N, product (P) depends upon the number (s_1) of machines of various vintages (m_1) in a designated neighbor-

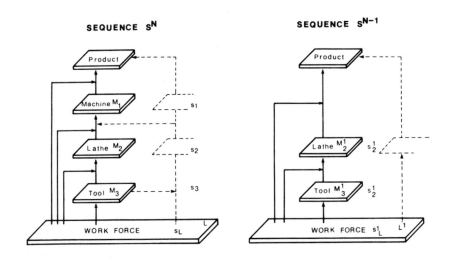

Figure 1-1. Two Production Sequences

hood ("factory") along with the labor force out of s_L allocated to this activity. In this instance, one could use machine specifications in a literal way to form the rule. Some indication of "complexity" is given by the organization of the figure, but complexity comparisons, as between S^N and S^{N-1}, or complexity measurement requires the reductions given in Chapter 3. Nevertheless, various economic measurements can be accomplished by taking a "census" across a lamination or by recording "time series" for a model history of transitions. These data can be used as inputs to conventional econometric analyses. (Analytical and econometric subroutines are routinely built into the representational model and provide a convenient form of data output.)

The tool-space and production-space functions can be operated in a variety of modes. For example, one can mechanistically use the operating rules cited earlier to drive the system to its maximum production level and then observe accompanying sociological interactions; or one can incorporate optimization calculations in the system to govern rates of tool-making and overall rates of production. In this instance, the cost of tools in terms of food and the price of food in terms of "final product" can be introduced as boundary conditions, and the demographic unit would adjust its operations accordingly.

Subtype 2: Hierarchical Production Submodels. Extending these lines of analysis, one could operate through tool-lathe-machine-final-product chains or longer sequences. The choice between longer (more redundant) chains and shorter chains could again be an outcome of optimization reactions to boundary prices.

The explicit representation of reswitching in choice of technique is but one of a number of capital-theoretic and production-theoretic concepts that can be directly represented in this fashion. A few illustrative examples should be noted:

(1) Widening the neighborhood of the production regime corresponds to broadening the domain of production interactions, such as occurs with improved transportation and communications systems.

(2) Labor force quality differences can be handled by stipulating appropriate variations in the production function and enlarging the labor force state space to include skill and experience categories which, in turn, depend on past employment or "education."

(3) Externalities can be explicitly modeled; e.g., greater deterioration of land could accompany use of hierarchical production techniques or extended production neighborhoods—that is, the superstructure of industrialization in higher laminations interacts to influence the "human" level below.

(4) One can use the fact that the model gives a complete count of all machines of all vintages to experiment with procedures for capital measurement or aggregation.

These suggestions as to model variants and elements are offered in order to communicate some idea of the range of SUR. It should be kept in mind that the rules can be built up with direct, descriptive, empirical information of the machine handbook type; that the processes work themselves out within an explicit locational frame; and that the complexity of a production process and its related social institutions is out in the open (and through theorems to be described, subject to measurement). SUR builds on individual actions and thus decomposition at the ultimate level. Although one can model a system in which all interactions are going at once—the demographic plane stewing while production plans mount—it is also possible to segment and compartmentalize the modeling, e.g., focusing on a particular set of rules and transitions for production relationships while constraining the demographic sector to relative inaction.

Practical Considerations: Some Concluding Comments and Conjectures

This chapter leaves many questions unanswered and invites skepticism. After all, we have only considered representational potentialities. We have not touched on the practical issues of what is involved in the actual mounting of an SUR program, what cost advantages or disadvantages the approach may have, and whether a particular problem might be better handled with an established heuristic or econometric technique. Some comments are required at this point.

In Chapter 2 we will review actual computational experience, but it must be noted that this experience only represents the merest testing of a few of the potentialities previously described. No full-scale finished studies are involved. There is insufficient data to make a cost analysis of the technique or a proper comparison between SUR and other established heuristic methods as to feasibility or strengths in particular applications. Despite this caveat, there is justification in proposing that serious attention be given to the technique—both for applied and for theoretical work. The arguments are recapitulated in the paragraphs that follow.

Applied Representations

The materials of this chapter demonstrate that it is possible to program at the level of the individual microunit. In this mode of analysis, each microunit is specified as an automaton oriented to all similar automata and to automata representing (severally) aggregates and various associations and artifacts. Whether this is a useful way to proceed depends upon a number of factors.

System Intricacy. First, there is the question of the difficulty of analysis. It is entirely possible that "interesting" societies are so intricate that an attempt to detail the significant interactions of the individual in such societies is doomed to frustration. This, of course, is a problem in virtually all social science research. One is forced toward abstractions, condensations, and simplifications by the nature of the material and by the limitations of the analytical tools at hand. A minimal claim here is that SUR is a tool which allows the analyst to take a closer look at detailed structure. It may be that the system will be found to be too intricate for meaningful analysis or that the problem of detailed structure is considered less interesting than the topics and problems which are susceptible to standard analysis. Even so, the reader should remain alert to a few qualifications and lines of procedure.

Some interesting social systems (and subsystems) appear to be effectively representable in near-full detail. Primitive economics, peasant villages, and ghetto subsystems fall into this category; obviously, if these are areas of interest, SUR becomes a strong candidate technique. However, one may not have a deep interest in such systems, yet a degree of success in representing them justifies giving attention to the theoretical implications of the modeling technique.[d]

Even where the intricacy of the system defeats practical modeling, there may still be something to be learned from even fragmentary or exploratory analysis. For example, the pilot cases discussed in Chapter 2 suggest that extremely intricate (and realistic) model behavior can be generated parsimoniously by a relatively small set of modeled behaviors. Conjectures rather than firm analyses are involved here, but one gets an impression that systems that call for hundreds of standard aggregate behavioral equations are representable by a much smaller number of behavioral rules operating on microunits described as automata. There may be good reasons to avoid an explicit SUR approach; for example, the topic of concern might be parameters of market demand or of investment behavior. These constructs might be susceptible to direct analysis whereas the underlying (automata) elements are known to be intricately interlocked in ways that do not greatly affect the parameters of interest. Even so, it may be worth some experimentation with incompletely specified reference SUR models, if only to discover how the data and behaviors in question might be generated by primitive elements.

Alternate Model Types. The last conjecture opens the door to a general area of concern, namely that modeling is usually performed for a purpose and the objective, whether positive or normative, may not require specification of smallest units and may be reasonably well satisfied by standard analysis. There can be no quarrel on this score; clearly if the requirements of a problem can be met effectively by a particular analysis, that should suffice. There have been any number of detailed planning studies and activity-analysis applications which have

---

[d]The word "primitive" must be used with caution. Individuals living in primitive economies may have extremely rich social and cultural lives. Direct social and economic interactions may be representable but the quality and nuances of cultural life appear to be well beyond the scope of SUR.

produced useful results in the domain that we have been examining, and these can stand on their own. There are, however, two points worth considering: (1) that many descriptive activity-analysis applications can be viewed as components of a larger SUR system (although not formally presented as such) and (2) that aspects of many planning models might be modified constructively by using an explicit SUR design. A few comments will elucidate these points.

On the matter of existing activity-analysis applications, it should be recognized that any model that operates in discrete time to calculate a distinct, finite output state from a given input state is, by definition, an automaton. For example, the automata in a national input-output analysis are industries. The input states are resource endowments and demand vectors, the output states are output production vectors, while the transition function is given by the inverse matrix or solution routine. The solution, however, is calculated as if all relevant adjustments occurred during the calculating interval, and so the real-time meaning of the calculating interval is not always clear. The suggestion here is that by examining explicit automata models for specific industries, aggregates of industries, or subaggregates one may obtain useful information about the dynamic setting of the processes which are condensed in the input-output solution. Some steps along these lines are taken in solution methods that involve decompositions or sequential organization of the model structure. But explicit automaton treatment as a "style" of analysis may produce structural or dynamic insights that could otherwise be overlooked.

This line of comment has particular cogency when we consider models with strong normative elements, that is, models which are operated in a planning mode or with strong optimization criteria or controls (i.e., static optimization systems solved by linear, nonlinear, or integer programming; dynamic optimization models solved by dynamic programming; large systems of either type solved through decomposition methods of various types). A generalization over such models is that they incorporate a concept of economic time appropriate for system solutions; that is, the models operate with a built-in computational adjustment period for which a general-equilibrium solution is calculated. Economists have tended to be circumspect in their use of equilibrium reasoning and in their specification of adjustment periods and out-of-equilibrium behavior.[e] Nevertheless, there are definite conceptual problems involved in operating with a general-equilibrium framework which are not necessarily relieved by specifying deep and intricate lag structures in the analytical system.

Again, the issue may be very much a matter of style and the way in which

[e]See, for example, F. Zeuthen, *Economic Theory and Method*, Cambridge, Mass., Harvard University Press, 1955 for a detailed study of relationships between abstract theoretical formulations and real structures and institutions. I think one has to be impressed by the skill and art which are required to fit model time to real time. The econometric and heuristic literatures contain very few examples of uncraftsmanlike work in this regard. Lag structure, adjustment, and adaptation have been primary analytical subjects of many of the most innovative economic and econometric scholars.

problems are formulated rather than a matter of mathematical form.[f] Model construction where there is a strong general-equilibrium motif can be dominated by implicit solution requirements and the need to tailor assumptions and constructions to a solvable equation of state. The cellular-automaton style seems less restrictive. Market balance and pricing conditions can be written into the system as in any of the standard modeling formats, or they can be calculated outside the system (e.g., in a distinct market place or planning-computation secretariat) and returned to the system as altered boundary conditions. Thus one can operate a "primitive" peasant-economy model with intricate and detailed ethnographic and demographic interactions and "separate" these behaviors from the "market."

To be specific, the peasant households and villages produce agricultural output according to social, demographic, and technical conditions, in response to standard economic variables (prices, realized incomes) and in response to controls (tax rates, directives, subsidies, etc.). The computational apparatus needed to solve for the economic variables and for policy-effective levels of the controls can be quite simple as compared to the apparatus needed to determine systemwide equilibrium values that take into account all variables and behaviors. In brief, the cellular-automaton style of analysis calls for descriptive, quasi-empirical study of computed model histories where some economic variables are constrained to equilibrium adjustments but other variables are allowed to propagate their own life stories.

To accentuate the positive, one could say that real economies and control systems tend to operate this way: that general equilibrium is really an economist's concept applying only to a subset of all variables of interest; that the sociological variables operate in a less restrictive regime and interact weakly with the economic conditions, and, furthermore, that only the economic variables are effectively under direct control.

This means, in effect, that using SUR, one works with a large-scale interactive system that would be prohibitively expensive to solve generally but is relatively low-cost when operated in a simulating mode. Model behaviors are examined by quasi-empirical methods such as econometric or spectral analysis of model-generated data—but where paths of the model are under simulated policy or social

---

[f]Note that the dynamic behavior of a cellular-automata model is formally describable by a set of difference equations (although the actual equations may be difficult to prespecify). Model histories are generated from boundary conditions, an input signal, and an initial configuration of cell states. Since the model operates in discrete time steps, it is by definition a difference equation system. Lag structures, however, can be quite intricate. Systemwide variables such as prices and value measures can be associated with standard difference-equation forms such as cobweb behavior and regular distributed lag response; but other factors and effects which operate over smaller cellular neighborhoods will propagate over the cellular field in a less predictable fashion. For example, a particular initial cell state can influence the state of a "distant" cell many periods later, but the period of influence depends upon the path of propagation through the cellular space and thus can be intricate indeed.

control. It is obvious that this mode of analysis can be low in cost relative to a simultaneous-equation analysis that subsumes the same behaviors. It is another question as to whether such behaviors are of interest.

Theoretical Concerns

The previous discussions point up characteristics that should be kept in mind when reviewing the simulation experience described in Chapter 2. Thus far we have been concerned only with characteristics that relate the SUR approach to other simulation, empirical, and quasi-empirical modes of analysis. It is time to remind the reader again of the implications of this work to lines of theoretical analysis. If one accepts the description of economic agents and units as automata—and the purpose of detailing representational potentialities and experiences is to make that description plausible—then a set of theorems and results applying to abstract automata transfers to automata representing socio-economic elements. Those results bearing on complexity measurement, exist-ence, and solvability enrich both representational quasi-empirical analysis and pure theory.

Appendix 1A:
The Game of Life—A Recreational Example

In the game of Life, the neighborhood of cell j is defined as the eight cells orthogonically and diagonally adjacent to it. A representation of this neighborhood is given by the *template* illustrated in Figure 1A-1a. The neighborhood is oriented to the cross-hatched cell. In effect, one slides the template from cell position to cell position during the time interval between $t - 1$ and t, and on the basis of cell states in the neighborhood at $t - 1$, one calculates the state of the cell in t. The transition function is given by the following rules:

1. Live cells with one or zero live neighbors *die* (of exposure).
2. Live cells with two or three live neighbors *survive.*
3. Live cells with four or more live neighbors *die* (of suffocation).
4. Quiescent cells with exactly three live neighbors are *born.*

This particular scheme, which has extraordinarily rich implications, was developed by the Cambridge mathematician R. Conway and popularized through Martin Gardner's *Scientific American* column on mathematical recreations.

A simple way to track life processes is to use ordinary graph paper. One plots the initial configuration as dots and then applies the death rules. Cells that will die are crossed out, and births are represented next with circles. (See Figure 1A-1.) The new generation will be the survivors plus the births—the dots plus the circles. One sees immediately that the one- or two-cell figures in b are too small to survive and that the three-cell figure in c oscillates indefinitely. Certain figures d to g are "stable," and it is possible to pack regions of the space with such clusters h. The dangers of congestion can be demonstrated in this last example. Imagine that a migrant enters the community and settles at the position marked with an "X." The resulting process of destruction and flight has impressed observers with its resemblance to urban decay (or viral infection).

The pattern given in i is called a "glider": experimentation shows that it moves across the field suggesting a pattern of migration. The pattern illustrated in j is a "glider generator." A glider generator and its offspring simulate a growing population. Observation of interactive ensembles of growing, migrating and oscillating forms is one of the pleasures of "life."

52

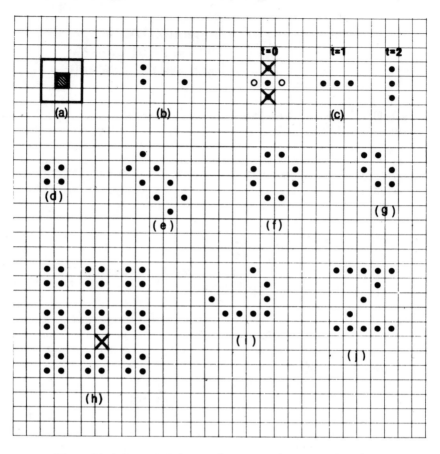

Figure 1A-1. Basic Cellular Configurations (Conway's Rules)

Appendix 1B:
A Simple Multilaminar
Model

We illustrate a multilaminar space with an extremely simple case using Conway's rules for the population plane. We label the cluster in Figure 1A-1d as a "tribe"; this is one of the two smallest units which can survive without growth, oscillation, migration, or decay. It is immaterial how one conceives of the individual cell elements—they could be thought of as persons or, perhaps, as extended families. A set of rules whereby such a grouping produces and accumulates capital is illustrated in Figure 1B-1 and described below. First, a neighborhood is defined: Figure 1B-1a is a "template" or pattern which is oriented to the cross-hatched cell, a representation of c_{kj} in capital space and c_{pj} in population space. Where the template is moved through the population space, it describes the production neighborhood C_{pj} of c_{kj}. Now we introduce a rule to produce capital if the template "fits" the community, and an additional rule to govern the aging and accumulation of capital.

Rule 1. If three live cells are in C_{pj}, a unit of capital is created at C_{kj}; the unit of capital is given the state index "4," indicating its useful life. [The creation of a unit of capital is illustrated in Figure 1B-1b; the cell with the index "4" is c_{kj}.]

Rule 2. Each live capital cell in year t is shifted one unit to the right in $t + 1$; its orientation is turned -90 degrees and its index reduced. [Figure 1B-1c shows the position after 4 "years," at which point a "steady state" is reached—a sustainable capital stock of four units is obtained from the "economic surplus" of the tribe.]

The rules are not restricted to the particular block-tribal configuration illustrated in Figure 1B-1a to c. Figure 1B-1d shows a tribe (an oscillating cluster) that is "ineffective" in production—that is, the given template cannot produce a "fit" in the population plane. The tribe illustrated in Figure 1B-1e can produce an interesting result. If we slightly change the rules and allow the capital neighborhood to be offset from the population neighborhood, we can reach the position illustrated in Figure 1B-1f. This tribe is more "efficient" than the original block formation (where efficiency is measured as output of capital per population element). Clearly, certain production regimes are most efficient for particular arrangements of population; and, conversely, particular population arrangements will call for the design of appropriate production technology. Obviously, this is a naive example designed for purposes of demonstration and not for serious analysis.

54

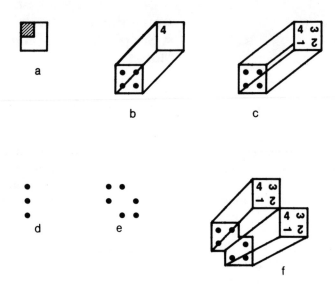

Figure 1B-1. Simple Production of Capital

2

Simulation Experience

The sketch of representational potentialities in the preceding chapter was intended to give the reader some idea of the types of behavior that could be handled within SUR. At this point it will be useful to review some actual simulation experience and some experience with model design.

The model that we will consider first was operated at Berkeley on large CDC machines under the direction of the author and A. Hoggatt. The model was programmed in FORTRAN as an independent-study project by two undergraduate computer science majors M. Katz and C. Dore. Both made considerable contributions to model design and carried out substantial tests of model function and performance. The basic programming was completed in less than an academic quarter and posed no significant problems. The experience suggests that the programming of an interesting and challenging empirically based system involves a minor expenditure of time as compared to other conventional heuristic formats.

It is not entirely clear why this should be so. We surmise that if correct initial choices are made in the design of the basic model, the resulting system involves a relatively small number of rules but a large number of potential system states. Rule changes and modifications involve adding "layers" of detail but do not usually invalidate previous constructions nor do they require extensive reprogramming of what went before. This may be a matter of luck or art in the design of the particular pilot models used, but we were impressed by the ease with which we could respecify behaviors or add more and more behaviors and lines of interaction to the system.

The focus was on testing the feasibility of a wide variety of types of representation and of various types of embedded data analysis. No attempt was made to obtain what one might label "definitive positive results." Nevertheless, a considerable number of "policy simulations" were themselves simulated, and the technique appeared ready for implementation in the LDC policy fields of technology planning for agriculture; birth control and demographic planning; tax-system analysis; and manpower/education planning. Some price and value concepts were used in the simulations, and these were easily integrated into the system; the model, however, was basically oriented to ethnographic description and to non-market planning applications.

Pragmatic lessons were of the following types. (1) The system operates well on a very large computer that permits immediate (virtual) storage of state spaces. (2) It is useful to build econometric subroutines into the basic program so that

55

one can produce data output in the form of simulated econometric analyses. (3) Output flexibility is helpful, particularly if one can shift fluidly from microfiche to graphics to hard copy. (4) It is good practice to build experimental designs into the simulation runs (e.g., subdivide the basic state field into a number of distinct state fields running under separate conditions).

A Primitive Agricultural Economy:
Simulation Experience

The basic state space for this model was a 21 by 21 array for "extended families" (as defined earlier) and a parallel lamination designating "land" (4 plots by 21 by 21, i.e., four plots of land per family location). Additional laminations stored information on production and family movements and past interfamily transactions. A rule structure similar to that given in the first part of Chapter 1 was employed. The family-state index was defined as the age structure of its members (supplemented with information about past history), and the land-state index was defined as the fertility level of plots (e.g., the maximum yield in bushels for operation with a predetermined number of workers).[a]

A model run was started by embedding a few families within the state space. The reproduction rules were set initially at the biological maximum for fecundity; and the individual families grew rapidly in size, depleted their land, and then split up to cultivate neighboring plots. The population space was quickly saturated, and since the land fertility parameters were set for austerity, population was restricted by "starvation" in the dependent categories. In adjusting to the harsh environment, families "decided" to pursue all options open to them: sharing of labor to optimize production, fertilization of plots, family mergers to merge land, and others. (In most runs the Malthusian checks were allowed to operate; but in other tests the birthrate was made a function of the household income, or a critical income level had to be reached before marriage and childbearing could begin. The modeled social controls checked population in a more humane way.) The model stabilized within a comparatively short period of time in the sense that over long model histories, total population fluctuated within bounds as did an aggregate index of land fertility. Similar bounds applied to variation in *vital statistics* (birthrates, death rates), *economic statistics* (e.g., production per worker, production per plot, percent of plots cultivated, percent of income transferred to hired labor, and so forth), *social statistics* (percent of families that move, percent of families that attempt merger, percent that succeed).

---

[a]This turns out to be a rectangular isoquant production function on each plot. The number of plots under cultivation can be varied, however, so that factor intensity for a four-plot unit is not fixed. In addition, since land productivity varies with use, the model is quite rich in its production characteristics. Cobb Douglas or CES functions could equally well have been used in modeling the system, but this seemed ostentatious at the time.

Stability in this sort of system is best left without precise definition. For example, we discovered that the model could be set so that all the statistics remained within the same range for an indefinitely long future despite various shocks. Alternatively the specification could be such that a particular constellation of social conditions would remain stable for particular initial conditions but would change with shocks. Alternatively, the physical world might change slowly but inalterably (as with wasteland rules), so that particular social structures might retain intact but population density might be subject to trend. Each of these possibilities involves different but operationally valid concepts of stability.

At all times cell-to-cell variation in demographic and land-fertility states was considerable, but as the model appeared to stabilize, the range of variations in state indices reduced. Changes in the basic rules led to predictable changes in system behavior in the stable state (e.g., less fertile land led to smaller families and higher average death rates), but some effects were difficult to foresee and at times surprising. (For example, effects of reduced land fertility on the rate of labor sharing or effects of altered sharecrop contracts on the pattern of cultivation were very much dependent on institutional or physical preconditions.[b]) This is as things should be; a heuristic approach should be susceptible to producing nontrivial information.

Many model generations have been computed, and the experimentation has shown the feasibility of representing a wide range of agricultural technologies and testing conjectures as to social implications of technological change within the model framework. The model has been operated using a rule structure including biological-maximum fecundity rates which were modified to approximate actual birthrates by social institutions and economic conditions. In addition, a wide range of ethnographic conditions were successfully incorporated within test runs, as was the possibility of representing surplus accumulation above a basic agricultural technology.

On the methodological front, the model has been operated to produce maps of the various state spaces and records of all social and economic transactions both completed and attempted (e.g., a family seeks out free labor within its immediate neighborhood but does not find it). State-space conditions have been analyzed through standard descriptive statistics (e.g., distributional parameters for family size or for land fertility) or through econometric techniques (e.g., estimated production-function parameters over land and labor force subsamples). Time series and time-series plots for major variables (income per land, birthrates, death rates, various distributional parameters, etc.) have been produced as regular output along with spectral analyses of the series, impact multipliers, and simulations of econometric analyses of the data output.

The major methodological problem remaining is to perfect practical criteria for judging model performance, e.g., tolerance limits for identifying rest states,

---

[b]Model variations were chosen to test the feasibility of using the framework for policy simulation in areas of agricultural or demographic planning and LDC public finance.

significantly different input multipliers, significantly different derived parameters, significantly different cross-sectional or time-series variances, etc. This is a difficult research area, and as is known from other heuristic studies, one that is plagued by issues requiring judgment.[c]

Finally, it must be recalled that despite these many references to statistical measures and econometric estimation over sets of output data, the system itself is completely deterministic. The resemblance of typical state-space transitions to Markov state-space transitions is striking; and a topic for active research and general questioning is the issue of whether transitions typically labeled as stochastic may, in fact, be deterministic at an identifiable fundamental level. (A topic which cannot be considered at length within these notes is that of "identifying a pattern" within the data. How, for example, should one classify a case in which the same "people" interact but in a different location?)

Urban Simulation

In another current application, pilot work has begun on a simulation of social deviance, including drug addiction, within an urban ghetto. This is a dramatically different type of representation, and the analysis is best approached through consideration of its component submodels, e.g., complexes of related transition rules. The basic cellular unit is again a family unit—in this case, the household. The basic state index is again a distribution of age categories. In this instance, however, a more detailed age structure for the teenage years is specified. There will be no more than one individual in a particular youth division (no twins), and each youth is described by a vector of demographic and economic characteristics, including sex, educational level, labor force experience, drug experience, voluntary associations, criminality, mental disturbance, and others. For example, a household unit might consist of two preteenage children, three individuals in critical youth divisions (a thirteen-year-old, a sixteen-year-old, and an eighteen-year-old), one mother, and one stepfather. The characteristics vector for the sixteen-year-old might, for example, specify male, twelfth-year reading level, no work, no hard drugs, youth gang member, arrest record, no mental disturbance, . . .

The transition functions involve own, family, block, neighborhood, and city relationships. For example, the reading-level state index would depend upon (past reading level, drug state, and gang membership), (educational level of family members, educational levels of the block peer group), (work experience among the members of the next oldest groups). The drug addiction state index

[c]The system is to be completely reprogrammed in APL to better handle analyses of model behavior and to offer greater flexibility and range in respresentation. FORTRAN versions are nevertheless reasonable testing media for a variety of conjectures on the economic and social characteristics of primitive agricultural economics.

would depend upon (the "own" state), (the educational level of the individual relative to that of actual labor force entrants), (the proportion of peer-group addicts within the block), (the number of active workers within the locale), and other variables.

The model will be used to represent a number of behavior syndromes which are difficult to specify analytically or in standard econometric formats because of complex interactions and the lack of a complete set of data for any one location. Data from a variety of different sources and locales will be used to develop rule structures for a number of different standard or "reference" neighborhoods. The model will be used to represent standard epidemiological processes, but its most critical use will be in representing specific poverty and subemployment characteristics—for example, distinguishing among income sources (welfare, low-paying transient jobs, hustling, etc.), distinguishing among household types (two parents, female-headed, dependent children, etc.), distinguishing among various qualities of past drug experience and social deviance, and distinguishing among various regulatory, educational, police, and therapeutic approaches applied to the drug population and to the general population. Preliminary analysis has confirmed that the formats of existing microdata sets are well approximated by the outputs of the experimental SUR model.

The model will also be used for policy simulations in which boundary conditions will be varied to correspond to differing conditions in the blue-collar and secondary labor market, to different welfare or social service programs, and to different regulatory or educational-therapeutic approaches. The model can thus be used to provide indirect tests of hypotheses concerning the social effects of different techniques of income maintenance or job creation, different labor market conditions, and different regulatory and educational approaches. Examination of these matters previously has been a matter of pure conjecture. The difference between pure and refined conjectures lies in the possibility of qualitative tests of syndromes within a complete logical structure and the possibility of fixing a fair number of the processes involved with actual and meaningful data.[d] As in other heuristic applications, one is using what is essentially a theoretical technique, the elaboration of numerical examples based on hypothetical data and parameters. One makes a claim for reasonableness of the application according to one's use of parameter values that correspond to observation.

Tipping Points

A forerunner application of CA reasoning can be found in a recently published analysis of racial "tipping points." Here Schelling made implicit use of a

[d]We note finally that the model contains a number of threshold phenomena: youth gangs require a "critical mass," and households with particular composition "move" in response to the deterioration of their neighborhood. These are typical case study phenomena but are rarely formalized. The final section considers other examples of such phenomena.

cellular-automata framework by proposing what is essentially a deterministic neighborhood-effect model subject to random shocks.

The key points of the Schelling construction are that the individual household reacts to the presence of another racial type within a predefined neighborhood. The tipping point can be defined as a percentage—variously (or simultaneously) as 50 percent in a one-block radius and/or 70 percent in a two-block radius and/or 75 percent in a three-block radius. "A cell flees if the tipping point is reached in its neighborhood." The Schelling variant contains a simple boundary condition—that those who flee are replaced by the other race—and that is sufficient to drive the system from a given initial distribution of households by racial type. All that is necessary to develop general flight is for a tipping point to be exceeded in the neighborhood of a particular cell and for the replacement cell to cause tipping in still other cell neighborhoods.

The mechanics of the process are quite simple, but the resultant dynamic pattern viewed as a time sequence in state maps appears to be quite dramatic. Again, it should be mentioned that in viewing the summary time-series statistics of flight, one is inclined to describe the process as a dynamic stochastic sequence; yet the example shows a simple deterministic integer process at the base. [See the case of Figure 1A-1h which demonstrates just such a process with the "Life" rules.]

The simple Schelling process is quite easily embellished. For example, the process can be run over initial conditions that include topographical features. A broad highway or a neutral feature such as a park or public building easily can be written into the state space and may cause a break in the chain reaction so that "neutral zone" racial boundaries appear. In other applications, one can show the inhibition of tipping points where flight also depends on available vacancies in "refuge" neighborhoods or where a property-value variable intervenes. Tipping functions or critical thresholds can also be established on other characteristics, as in the drug addiction example; and, of course, the tipping characteristic can be incorporated in more general urban models which also specify a wide range of social and economic behaviors—some of which interact with the tipping phenomenon.

A Planning Extension

The Schelling model has been elaborated and set into an explicit cellular-automata framework by K. Vandell in work carried out at M.I.T. under the direction of B. Harrison. This model leads in a quite different direction from those previously discussed. In fact, the SUR representation in this case develops into a practical tool for the urban planner, developer, regional analyst, and others. The first stage of the M.I.T. analysis has been completed and consists of brief simulation experience in a model which incorporates a variety of behavioral functions of standard type (supply-and-demand functions for real estate, reaction functions based on price and value data, etc.) which have cell states as their argument. The core of the model is a cellular-automaton model where the primary cell consists of a household and housing unit which can assume states according to the following scheme (illustrated in Appendix 2A):

Income level (four states)

Race (two states)

Employment location index (corresponds to having neighborhoods defined in initial conditions)

Neighborhood index (corresponds to having neighborhoods defined in initial conditions)

Housing type (four states)

Initial value of house (five states)

Quiescent state (defined as a vacant unit under any of the housing-type categories)

The basic style of simulation is to establish an initial configuration corresponding to a distribution of household-family conditions over a cellular space. Certain constellations of relatively homogeneous conditions are identifiable as housing neighborhoods, e.g., a ghetto occupied by poor blacks in multifamily, low-value houses; a white, middle-class, single-family neighborhood; mixed housing-stock neighborhoods, and so forth. Experimenter control over how the initial cell states are assigned and how the housing neighborhoods are configured can be thought of as equivalent to either a statistician's selection of a sample area or a planner's arrangement of a development complex on a planning board. In the latter instance, one can lay out the board using empirical (e.g., census) data and even topographic features which might affect patterns of neighborhood formation. Table 2A-1 illustrates a standard neighborhood arrangement used in the M.I.T. simulations. Ghetto extension is illustrated along with proposals for a superhighway and park that cut the neighborhood. These last features (not in the present system) could be represented by special cell states and a new set of transition rules governing reactions to these special states, e.g., upward (downward) shifts in the demand curves for housing according to proximity to the park (highway).

In the stereotyped simulation, the model is stimulated by immigration of blacks into the core ghetto. By varying conditions in the market functions, in the topographical features, or in preexisting states, one can control (or predict) tendencies toward tipping or toward stabilizing segregated or integrated housing patterns.

Conclusions

This section on operating models is short on final results. Most of the research described here is just entering the active stage, and published pragmatic findings are not to be expected for several years. Nevertheless, it may be hoped that the descriptions given here will be sufficient to prompt additional applied study and also encourage readers to give some credence to the theoretical conjectures that follow. A point to be stressed is that in using the technique for model-building, one runs into very few practical obstacles and one can easily concentrate on the subject rather than on the method. Nevertheless, the method has proved itself so fascinating that the author and his associates have tended to test out as many different simulating and representational frameworks as possible.

Appendix 2A:
Simulation of Racial Tipping

The diagrams illustrate, respectively, laminations representing family income, neighborhood, housing type, housing value, and race for the initial year and "race" three model iterations later. The numbers indicate state levels of the variables. The outlined subarea is the ghetto. The overlay in the "neighborhood" indicates the proposed path for a "superhighway" and a location for a "park" (not in Vandell and Harrison). "Market functions" compute prices, and the model simulates house-purchase transactions and migration. The resultant pattern of social behavior is described by Vandell and Harrison as follows.

The resultant expansion conforms to expected patterns. Since the wealthier blacks tend to move first, they would seek out housing in the middle-upper-middle-class or working-class neighborhoods. The poor white neighborhood contains housing stock which is of value too low to be considered by them. Thus the upper-middle-class and working-class neighborhoods receive the bulk of the black outmigration. The very poor white neighborhood receives only 12.5 percent. Although the upper-middle-class neighborhood receives 37.5 percent of the black outmigration, this is into homes bordering the black neighborhood which are of comparatively moderate value–$21,200, $20,100, and $19,600 initially. Movement into the working-class white neighborhood claimed homes valued at $13,100 and $18,500, $15,666 and $17,600 initially. Finally, movement into the poor neighborhood claimed a home initially valued at $13,100, which was the highest-value home in that neighborhood.
   The tipping mechanism accounted for two out of eight total incidents of racial transition during the three time intervals studied, while blockbusting accounted for the remaining six. Tipping also resulted in six site vacancies in the white neighborhoods created by white outmigration in anticipation of black invasion. In each case, however, black buyers could not be found at the asking price. Three of the six vacancies were in the poor white neighborhood. Unwillingness by the highest-income-potential black movers to inhabit the lower-quality stock in this neighborhood contributed to this situation.

The extended ghetto is seen as the bounded area of 0's in the final figure (race period 3). The 2's are the transitional units. We again note that the analysis could be replicated using actual planning maps and standard econometric reaction functions. "Parks" and "superhighway" could be simulated as policy interventions to check the tipping process.

Table 2A-1
Simulation of Racial Tipping

Family Income Period 0	Neighborhood Period 0	Housing Type Period 0
4 4 4 4 4 4 4 3 2 2 2 2 3 3 2	3 3 3 3 3 3 3 2 2 2 2 2 2 2 2	1 1 2 2 2 2 2 2 3 4 2 1 3 3 3
4 4 4 4 4 4 4 2 2 3 2 2 2 3 3	3 3 3 3 3 3 3 2 2 2 2 2 2 2 2	2 2 2 2 1 1 1 1 1 1 4 4 2 2 3
4 4 4 4 4 4 4 2 3 2 2 2 2 2 3	3 3 3 3 3 3 3 2 2 2 2 2 2 2 2	2 2 2 1 1 1 2 1 4 3 3 3 4 4 2
4 4 4 4 4 4 4 2 2 2 2 3 2 3 3	3 3 3 3 3 3 3 2 2 2 2 2 2 2 2	1 1 2 2 4 4 3 3 2 2 2 2 1 1 1
4 4 4 4 4 4 4 2 3 2 2 2 2 2 3	3 3 3 3 3 3 3 2 2 2 2 2 2 2 2	1 1 2 2 2 4 3 2 2 2 1 1 3 3 4
4 4 4 4 4 3 3 2 3 2 2 3 2 3 3	3 3 3 3 3 1 1 2 2 2 2 2 2 2 2	1 1 2 2 2 4 4 3 2 2 2 2 1 1 4
4 4 4 4 3 2 2 2 2 2 3 3 3 3 2	3 3 3 3 1 1 1 1 1 1 2 2 2 2 2	2 2 2 3 3 3 4 4 4 4 1 1 2 2 1
4 4 4 4 3 3 2 2 2 2 2 3 2 2 3	3 3 3 3 1 1 1 1 1 1 2 2 2 2 2	4 4 4 4 2 2 2 1 1 1 1 3 2 2 1
4 4 4 1 2 3 2 1 2 1 1 1 1 2 2	3 3 3 1 1 1 1 1 1 4 4 4 4 4 4	2 2 2 3 3 4 4 4 4 4 1 1 1 1 2
4 4 4 1 1 1 2 2 1 2 1 1 1 1 1	3 3 3 1 1 1 4 4 4 4 4 4 4 4 4	2 2 2 3 3 4 4 4 2 1 1 1 1 1 1
2 2 1 1 1 1 1 1 1 1 2 1 2 1 1	4 4 4 4 1 4 4 4 4 4 4 4 4 4 4	2 2 2 2 2 1 1 4 4 4 3 2 2 4 4
2 1 2 2 2 1 1 2 2 2 1 1 1 2 1	4 4 4 4 4 4 4 4 4 4 4 4 4 4 4	2 2 2 2 4 1 1 1 3 2 1 1 1 2 2
1 1 1 2 1 2 2 2 1 1 1 1 1 1 1	4 4 4 4 4 4 4 4 4 4 4 4 4 4 4	2 2 2 4 4 1 1 1 2 2 1 2 1 3 3
2 1 1 1 1 1 1 1 2 1 1 2 1 2 1	4 4 4 4 4 4 4 4 4 4 4 4 4 4 4	2 2 2 4 4 1 3 3 2 4 2 2 1 1 2
1 2 1 1 1 2 1 1 1 1 1 1 2 1 1	4 4 4 4 4 4 4 4 4 4 4 4 4 4 4	2 2 2 3 3 1 1 1 4 4 2 1 1 3 2

Housing Value Period 0	Race Period 0	Race Period 3
5 5 5 5 5 5 5 4 4 4 3 3 4 4 3	1 1 1 1 1 1 1 1 1 1 1 1 1 1 1	1 1 1 1 1 1 1 1 1 1 1 1 1 1 1
5 5 5 5 5 5 5 3 3 4 3 3 3 4 4	1 1 1 1 1 1 1 1 1 1 1 1 1 1 1	1 1 1 1 1 1 1 1 1 1 1 1 1 1 1
5 5 4 5 5 5 5 3 3 4 4 4 3 3 4	1 1 1 1 1 1 1 1 1 1 1 1 1 1 1	1 1 1 1 1 1 1 1 1 1 1 1 1 1 1
5 5 5 4 5 5 5 3 4 3 3 4 4 4 3	1 1 1 1 1 1 1 1 1 1 1 1 1 1 1	1 1 1 1 1 1 1 1 1 1 1 1 1 1 1
5 5 5 5 4 4 4 4 3 3 4 3 4 3	1 1 1 1 1 1 1 1 1 1 1 1 1 1 1	1 1 1 1 1 0 0 0 2 1 1 1 1 1 1
5 5 4 4 4 4 4 3 4 4 3 4 3 4 4	1 1 1 1 1 0 0 1 1 1 1 1 1 1 1	1 1 1 1 0 0 0 0 0 0 1 1 1 1 1
4 5 5 5 4 4 3 3 3 3 3 3 4 4 3	1 1 1 1 0 0 0 0 0 0 0 1 1 1 1	1 1 1 1 0 0 0 0 0 0 1 1 1 1 1
5 5 5 5 4 4 4 3 2 2 3 3 3 3 4	1 1 1 1 0 0 0 0 0 1 1 1 1 1 1	1 1 1 2 0 0 0 0 0 0 1 1 1 1 1
5 5 4 2 3 3 3 2 3 1 2 1 2 3 3	1 1 1 0 0 0 0 0 1 1 1 1 1 1 1	1 1 1 0 0 0 0 0 0 1 1 1 1 1 1
3 2 1 1 2 2 1 2 2 1 2 1 3 2 2	1 1 1 1 0 1 1 1 1 1 1 1 1 1 1	1 1 1 2 0 2 1 1 1 1 1 1 1 1 1
3 1 3 3 3 1 2 3 2 2 2 2 2 2 2	1 1 1 1 1 1 1 1 1 1 1 1 1 1 1	1 1 1 1 0 1 1 1 1 1 1 1 1 1 1
2 2 1 3 2 2 2 2 1 2 2 2 2 2 2	1 1 1 1 1 1 1 1 1 1 1 1 1 1 1	1 1 1 1 1 1 1 1 1 1 1 1 1 1 1
2 1 1 2 2 1 1 2 2 2 1 2 1 3 2	1 1 1 1 1 1 1 1 1 1 1 1 1 1 1	1 1 1 1 1 1 1 1 1 1 1 1 1 1 1
2 3 2 1 1 3 1 2 2 2 2 2 2 3 2	1 1 1 1 1 1 1 1 1 1 1 1 1 1 1	1 1 1 1 1 1 1 1 1 1 1 1 1 1 1

Part II:
Structural Analysis

Introduction to Part II

At this point we shift our perspective and consider the possibility of investigating socioeconomic structures through investigation of the structure of SUR models. Our first concern is the complexity dimension, and we will examine techniques for deriving parameters that measure degrees and qualities of complexity. The analysis takes us fairly deep into formal CA theory, and Chapter 3 gives a gloss of results and theorems that allow practical calculation of complexity parameters. The analysis, although complete in itself, suggests some original approaches to problems in capital theory and the theory of economic development. Accordingly, in Chapter 4 we will view some attempts to apply complexity analysis to the study of heterogeneous capital goods and infrastructure in developed economies. These topics are only a first step into theory based on the CA motif, and it is worth previewing some of the lines of study that will ultimately be considered.

Despite the fact that formal CA analysis has been in existence for less than a generation, the field contains an extraordinary range of theoretical constructs: fundamental theorems on the existence of particular abstract structures; theorems on computational algorithms, and theorems bearing on specific applications such as pattern recognition, description of neural networks, and ontogeny. In order to classify the materials of greatest potential interest to economists, this section presents a brief taxonomy of social science fields and styles of analysis which can borrow profitably from CA analysis. The ordering runs roughly from pragmatic and matter-of-fact applications to conjectural imagery.

The ordering also roughly corresponds to what might be labeled "degree of involvement" with the SUR approach. The first categories require little more than acceptance of SUR as one of a number of potentially useful simulation techniques. The later categories presume acceptance of close correspondence between real world phenomena and SUR counterparts. The categories are labeled as follows: (1) Theory of computations underlying SUR simulation, (2) production theory involving roundaboutness and structural complexity; (3) relationship between production techniques and social organization; (4) general-equilibrium, existence, and planning characteristics of systems made up of cellular automata; (5) econometric analysis of data drawn from CA systems; (6) relationship between size, complexity, and autarky, (7) theory of dialectic processes, (8) theory of signaling and the organization of planning systems, and (9) theory of decisions. We have already considered theory for the representational mode. Chapters 3 and 4 consider theory appropriate to complexity measurement in a model created specifically for its representational qualities. Subsequent chapters "extend the involvement" and delve into the latter categories.

3 Complexity Measurement

Chapters 1 and 2 show the practicality of representing an economic system as a computable composition of automata. The salient characteristics of the system, the SUR model, are the following:

1. Hierarchic organization of production with direct representation of such sequences as labor-tools-machines-product.
2. Representation of demographic and ethnographic interactions as interactions of an automaton with its neighbors; representation of group interactions as relationships of composite automata (where "neighborhoods" can represent various locational, social, or economic fields of interactions).
3. Computation of demand functions and other market and behavioral functions as output states of abstract automata depending upon the states of automata representing individuals and productive units.

The system allows representation of relationships at the very small microlevel with full display of interactions, but permits full-system integration of macrobehaviors and standard lines of aggregation.

This chapter begins the theoretical analysis of such systems, described intuitively as dynamic models with structure defined in terms of hierarchic relationships between and across laminations of like elements (machines, individuals, stocks of products, etc.). Our interest will be in examining the possibility of taking such a model and forming a quantitative assessment of the degree of "complexity" (left undefined for the moment) of the economic system it represents. This chapter requires no special mathematical prerequisites but is, nevertheless, dense with notations. The Appendix to the Introduction provides introductory materials that may clarify the exposition here.

In most cases one could build a working model using rules similar to those given in Chapters 1 and 2 without paying particular attention to structural characteristics. Standard programming experience is all that is needed to avoid such obvious mistakes as causing rules to depend on current states or building in an infinite enumeration of states (e.g., by allowing individual families to grow beyond all bounds or by recording an element's geneology within its state index). However, the interesting questions in model construction and interpretation concern the manner in which one "trades off" areas of complexity. A particular relationship might be represented through simple two-state elements operating through fairly intricate rules and neighborhoods; or, alternatively, the relationship might be represented through multistate elements and a less intricate rule and neighborhood structure.[a] For example, in the classic work of von Neumann, a simple five-cell neighborhood operated for the elements of his computing automata. His theorems were reformulated by his successors, using a larger neighborhood but a smaller number of states for each cell. Burks (1970) describes von Neumann's development of the cellular-automata model and later efforts in realizing it and extending its scope. The Burks volume also includes an extensive bibliography and a number of germinal essays. Of particular note are essays by Burks on the history of the concept, essays by Thatcher and Holland on computer-constructor universality, Moore's work on the "Garden of Eden," and highly original work by Ullam on extensions into cellular growth. Other seminal works are translations of the von Neumann problem by Codd (1968) and Smith (1971a,b); descriptions of *Slow Automata* (McNaughton, 1961b), and *probabilistic automata* (Rabin, 1963), (Shannon, 1953), and (von Neumann, 1956).

The trade-offs of complexity equivalences have, in fact, been formalized, so that one can actually measure the intrinsic complexity of a model regardless of its state, neighborhood, or rule complexity. Given a benchmark "simple model," the analysis gives order-of-magnitude equivalents (in terms of computer requirements) between a more intricate example and the benchmark referent.

This turns out to be an extremely important result for social science applications, which by their very nature involve intricate state specifications and a laminar neighborhood design. In addition, the trade-off relationships are of considerable usefulness in monitoring computer requirements during the design stage of applied modeling. For example, one might be operating with a working model of "village" demographic interactions. It might be desirable to include

[a]Mathematical development of CA theory involves the separate concepts of "simulation" and "representation." "Representation" evokes metaphorical or imagist content: thus a particular state index in von Neumann's first construction connoted a component function, perhaps the capability of recognizing the state of a neighboring cell, perhaps the capability of operating with other cells to perform as a Turing machine (itself a representation of a universal programmable computer). The whole of von Neumann's cellular automaton, a 29-state device, "represented" a universal computer-constructor, a system with universal computing capacity and the capability of working with "raw material" to produce exact copies of itself (which could, in turn, self-reproduce).

What is "represented" in a particular application will depend upon the interests, motivation, and problem orientation of the researcher. In contrast to this usage, "simulation" is understood as a form of expressing (proving) mathematical correspondence or equivalence. Thus a typical line of proof would show that an eight-state automaton configuration operating on a two-dimensional cellular space but specifying a larger neighborhood of interaction than the von Neumann automaton (nine cells against five) could *simulate* a von Neumann automaton. That is, the simulating automaton could produce identical outputs for relevant identical inputs (but might not preserve structural characteristics). The notion of "trade-off" is significant here. The simulation of an automaton with a large and complicated neighborhood by one with a simple neighborhood would be accomplished at a cost in state complexity and/or computing time. These "costs" provide the basis for direct measurement of the organizational complexity of the model system.

this submodel within a larger "regional" system in such a way that the entire submodel is approximated as a "cell" in the larger automata system. The "trade-off" theorems allow one to calculate the overall complexity of a macrosystem made up of components which are themselves complex; in turn, one has opened up a significant new line into what happens in the process of aggregation. We will return to other applications of complexity measurement subsequently; for the moment, it is sufficient to remind the reader that the complexity-measurement approach gives some index of the communications and information requirements of a physical system and also some indication of the system's breakdown potential. Three caveats should be issued at this time. First, there is not yet a body of experience with the theorems, so that their practicality is unknown. Second, the complexity measure applies to an abstract model used to represent the real world, not to the world itself. Finally, cultural elements in the system, its political economy, and its essential spirit may be unrepresentable. That is, we may be able to model a capitalist production system and a socialist production system but not be able to capture the elements that distinguish them as economies.

A Preview of the Analysis

Before launching the formal analysis, let us again review the type of system we shall be investigating and the type of question we shall ask. Consider the production process illustrated as sequence S^N in Figure 3-1. Workers, tools,

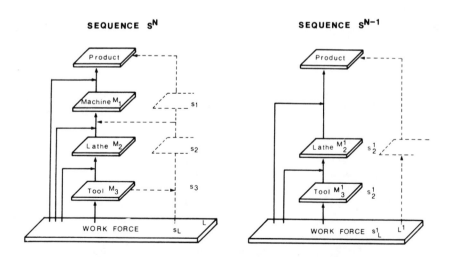

Figure 3-1. Two Production Sequences

lathes, machines, and final product (assembly) are represented as automata on separate laminations, while the arrows indicate the location of neighborhoods over which transition rules operate. The figure thus represents a situation in which the assembly of final product requires the production of components at the machining stage and an assembly labor force. The maintenance of a stock of machines requires a tool stage, and so on. The figure applies to a steady state sustainable technology. It abstracts from buffer stocks and/or "imports" of the intermediate "capital goods." It also abstracts for the moment from the complication that intermediate capital goods can themselves be produced at the end of a production chain. We note in passing that the "worker" lamination is itself an abstract representation of demographic cellular automata of the sorts discussed in the previous chapters.

Now compare S^N with the truncated sequence S^{N-1}; simple inspection of systems such as these prompts a number of questions. Do the two modes of organizing production result in qualitative or order-of-magnitude differences in communications requirements? Are there special investment requirements in such organizations? Is one mode more likely to appear in an underdeveloped country than some other? These questions are vague; the complexity-measurement approach offers opportunities to refine them, and we proceed toward a more rigorous analysis based on a body of formal theorems. In substance the theorems show the following:

1. The "complexity" of an economic system can be described by a vector of parameters $\vec{P}$ or by a single index of system complexity P.
2. The complexity parameters associate with characteristics such as the following:

   (a) *The range of interactions of individuals or individual components.* For example, an economy which employs large computers with a nationwide network of remote terminals would register a higher "range" parameter than an economy employing many small, self-contained machines.

   (b) *The extent of roundaboutness.* For example, an economy which depends upon a long chain of specialized functions such as a manufacturer, wholesaler, jobber, or dealer sequence would register a higher "hierarchy" index than would an economy in which the manufacturer sold directly to the public.

   (c) *The complexity of the individual unit.* For example: the individual computer in 2(a) would measure as more complex than the terminal and less complex than the large time-sharing machine; the manufacturer-seller in 2(b) would register as more complex than many of the individual elements in the chain.

   (d) *The intricacy of interactions.* For example, a bureaucracy with a five-page application form would register a higher index than one with two pages.

3. The complexity parameters associate with specific infrastructure, investment, and personnel needs. For example, 2(a), 2(b), 2(c), and 2(d) associate respectively with: (a) a need for a matching transportation/communications network; (b) an organizational and communications system; (c) differing requirements on an educational system; (d) a computing secretariat of prescribed size.

4. The complexity parameters are in the form of cardinal indices which can be used for a variety of descriptive and normative purposes—for example, comparing levels of economic development, computing infrastructure requirements, assessing external effects of technical change.

5. The complexity parameters can also be used for theoretical predictions, as, for example, in a judgment that technical change which involves increased specialization and "layering" of the system tends to impose greater infrastructural cost than does a movement toward more intricate interconnections among preexisting layers of production. Another line of inquiry is in the theoretical investigation of scale phenomena. A number of complexity measures depend directly on the range over which a system operates. Investigation of the behavior of such measures for several broad classes of descriptive model should bring insights as to the foundation reasons for scale economies or diseconomies.

Comments. The substance of these "theorems" still requires elucidation, and it will be helpful to continue the computer analogy.

Suppose we are comparing a machine labeled B which has an intricate bottom-level (input-output) subsystem with one labeled A which has an intricate organization of intermediate-level components (e.g., the comparison is between a commercial time-sharing system and a scientific computer). These characteristics should be quantifiable: at the very least, one could use engineering data on the number of standard components, connections, transistors, and chips needed to realize the overall design and specific design stage. These measures should allow some valid comparisons between the two machines. One moves to more meaningful comparisons if one can relate block subsystems of the two machines to some standard referent and record relative behaviors, e.g., the ability to handle more/less input data or the ability to influence more/fewer peripheral subsystems. As is commonly done in purchase comparisons, these types of performance measures are translated into machine attributes which can be the basis of dollars-and-cents decisions. Finally, one may wish to move even further and produce a measure of overall system complexity. This involves combining such attributes as range of influence over peripheral machines, intricacy of programming logic, and intricacy of connections within a particular chip; but the problem is solvable given a reference technology. For example, a particular switching function of a chip could be accomplished by an (older) reference technology through a particular configuration of relays, core space, amplifiers, and control mechanisms. The complexity measure of this reference configuration could then be used to provide a measure of the complexity embodied in the chip. By suitable reductions of all components, systems, and subsystems one could calculate the dimensions of a machine in the reference technology that would be capable of performing the comparison machine's functions. (The machine might, of course, be hopelessly unconstructable—as for example in an attempt to reproduce the functions of a CDC 7600 with the technology of an IBM 650.) In the example that we have been considering, the complexity measure could be the length of a string of abstract 650s needed to replicate the advanced machine performance; but it is more useful to take as the reference an abstract unit simply described as a cellular automaton.

In the process of such analysis, one finds that certain classes of behavior such as "the ability to operate in a time-sharing mode with M channels," "the ability to control particular construction activities," or "the ability to produce a replica of the machine itself" require the achievement of specific threshold levels of complexity measured in terms of the abstract automaton, or in terms of the dimensions of a reference type of machine. Such findings are the bread, butter, and marmalade of theoretical computer science inquiry.

Now let us go back to the economic questions. We are arguing that socioeconomic system block diagrams or SUR computer programs are, in effect, data equivalent to a description of a computer, and as such are susceptible to analysis of complexity characteristics. One can, for example, operate with a closed system of individual-family-village interactions and produce a measure of the "complexity" of a village. One could also ignore such low-level interactions and consider only the interactions of villages within a confederation. However, it is also possible to integrate the two analyses to produce a measure of total system complexity which embraces both intravillage interactions and the intricacy of relationships among villages. When a closer look is taken at the parameters produced, the analysis should also point up the types of social hardware and circuitry (infrastructure) needed to support system complexity. Clearly, this analogy should hold up as well through a consideration of types of production and economic relationship.

Formal Description of Laminar Models

We proceed by developing notations and definitions which represent a practical compromise between those used earlier and those found in the mathematical literature. The order of discussion is as follows. We first define a *uniform cellular space* (UCS) and a *cellular configuration*. These are the reference forms in the established mathematical literature. Economic models, however, contain special *boundary conditions*, such as land boundaries, market limits, resource limits, etc. Such models are also likely to be specified in laminar form, as was the practice in

Chapters 1 and 2. To relate the economic model to the standard reference forms, we need to show equivalence between typical boundary conditions and certain configurations. We also need to show an equivalence between laminar forms and the standard UCS. This last we do by showing that the laminar model is actually of a form labeled a *uniform laminar hierarchic cellular space* (ULHCS) and that a ULHCS can be reduced to an equivalent UCS.

Complexity measurements will be calculated for UCS forms, so that the full complexity of a system involves a composition of (1) the complexity required to reduce the system from ULHCS to UCS, (2) the additional state complexity needed for adjustment to boundary conditions, and (3) the inherent complexity of the system which depends upon the range of interactions of the individual cell (neighborhood conformation) and the inherent complexity of the cell unit (number of states assumed by the cell). Required first is a formal description of a uniform cellular space. (This notation elaborates that given in Notation 2 in the Appendix to the Introduction.)

A Uniform Cellular Space

(1) An infinite plane is divided into squares in checkerboard or latice fashion.

(2) A "copy" of a particular automaton [described implicitly by (3) to (7)] is embedded in each square. The square together with the automaton is labeled a *cell*.

(3) Associated with each cell is a (finite) *neighborhood* of m cells. It is most convenient to describe the neighborhood of the ith cell by a *template* which is oriented to the ith cell and designates those cells in the neighborhood.

(4) The state of cell i at time t is uniquely determined by a *transition function f* whose argument is the states of the m neighboring cells in $t - 1$.

(5) The number of distinct *states* associated with each automaton is restricted to V (finite). The cell states within a neighborhood are designated $(V^1, \ldots, V^m)$. V^0 is the state of the reference cell.

(6) The *quiescent state V_0* is distinguished and possessed by every automaton. The characteristic of the quiescent state is that

$$f(V_0^0, V_0^1, \ldots, V_0^m) = V_0^0$$

i.e., there can be no spontaneous generation of a nonquiescent state.

(7) Other than (6), f is unrestricted.

(8) Time proceeds according to a clock to which all cells are synchronized. At each time step all but a finite number of cells are in the quiescent state.

(9) The disposition of nonquiescent cells is labeled a *configuration* of cells. A configuration of cells with particular representational characteristics is termed a *model*.

Boundary Characteristics

The previous discussion permits a configuration of ν-state cells to be dispersed over an infinite checkerboard; this is the most general case. However, it is also possible to select a configuration so that all cellular activity takes place within a bounded region of the cellular space. This can be shown by a construction that establishes a new cell state, $V^0_{\nu+1}$, which is assigned to cells bordering a closed region of a cellular space to form a boundary. Cells close to the boundary may behave differently than cells in the interior of the closed region. Thus it is also necessary to assign new cell states to handle special boundary reactions. This construction is given by (1) to (3) as follows:

1. Expand the number of states to $\nu + 1$, such that

$$f(V^0_{\nu+1}, V^1, \ldots, V^m) = V^0_{\nu+1}$$

2. Locate cells in state $V_{\nu+1}$ to form the desired boundary.
3. Expand the number of cell states to $\lambda V + 1$, where the additional states are assigned by f according to whether the individual cell has $1, 2, \ldots, \lambda - 1$ boundary cells within its neighborhood.

In practice, the full expansion of states according to (3) will not be required. In any case, computer algorithms can be chosen to simulate the full construction. The economic models discussed in earlier sections can now be classified as configurations incorporating boundary conditions, but nevertheless a cellular automaton within the general description. A computer "simulation" of the sort described in earlier chapters is thus a simulation of a bounded region.

Uniformity

The CA economic models are examples of *uniform cellular automata*, a class of automata for which a great many significant results are proven. Intuitively, a uniform cellular automaton corresponds to a cellular space in which the same neighborhood template applies to each cell and does not change according to position on the field or with the passage of time or with a "dialectic" change in configurations. The basic theorems apply to uniform cellular spaces, so that this identification is important. One should also note that the theorems may not hold *within* a narrowly bounded configuration, but they are relevant for many models that can be simulated on large computers.

Properly speaking, the SUR models discussed in previous chapters fit the category of a uniform, hierarchic, laminar cellular space (ULHCS). The model is *hierarchic*, where automata on "upper" laminations have neighborhoods on the same or "lower" neighborhoods. It is "uniform" since the neighborhoods do not alter with position or time (i.e., the computer program simulating the cellular space does not change). This appears to be the most natural, intuitive, and convenient format for practical model-building, so that it is necessary at the very start to show that a ULHCS is equivalent to (or can be simulated by) a UCS. Hence we obtain the following.

THEOREM 3-1. A uniform hierarchic laminar model (where each lamination is a two-dimensional Euclidean plane) is reducible to a two-dimensional uniform cellular space. Complexity indices are computable (algorithms and procedures are given in the course of demonstrating the theorem). The theorem is demonstrated by construction. We distinguish three cases, proceeding from a restricted, uninteresting model to the most general case.

Case 1

A model consisting of separate laminations in which there are no cross-lamination interactions (e.g., all neighborhoods and reference cells are on the same lamination) can be reduced to a single lamination by a succession of *collapsing* moves.

Assume there are m_1, m_2, m_3, . . . live cell states on each lamination. Orient the first lamination to the second, and proceed by renumbering cell states on the second lamination so that the cell-state index will distinguish laminations. (See Figure 3-2.) This requires m_2 states where a live cell on the second lamination is oriented to a quiescent cell on the first; m_1 states where a live state on the first lamination is oriented to a quiescent cell on the second; $m_1 m_2$ states to cover the juxtaposition of live cells on each; and the quiescent state. Thus M_2, the number of states on the second lamination created by the collapsing move, is given by

$$M_2 = 1 + m_1 + m_2 + m_1 m_2$$

$$M_1 = 1 + m_1$$

$$\therefore M_2 = M_1 + m_2 M_1$$

We then collapse the new second lamination onto the third. By similar construction, M_3, the number of states on the third lamination created by the collapsing move, is given by

$$M_3 = M_2 + m_3 M_2$$

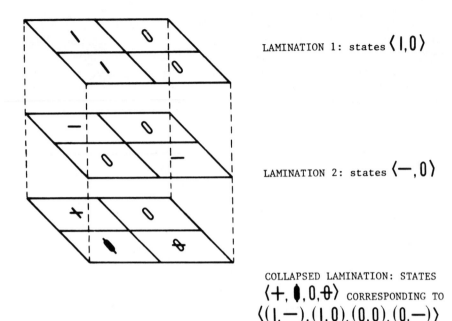

LAMINATION 1: states $\langle 1, 0 \rangle$

LAMINATION 2: states $\langle -, 0 \rangle$

COLLAPSED LAMINATION: STATES
$\langle +, \textbf{0}, 0, \oplus \rangle$ CORRESPONDING TO
$\langle (1, -), (1, 0), (0, 0), (0, -) \rangle$

Figure 3-2. Combining of Laminar Spaces (lamination 1 collapsed on lamination 2).

More generally, M_j, the number of states on the jth lamination given by a sequence of collapsing moves, is defined inductively by

$$M_j = M_{j-1} + m_j M_{j-1} = M_{j-1}(1 + m_j) \tag{3.1}$$

Neighborhoods. By tracing through the steps of the reduction, one also sees that the neighborhood on the collapsed cellular space will be the template formed as the outer boundary of the superimposed original templates.[b] For example, if the state of cell i on the Kth lamination is influenced by a cell N cells to the north and W cells to the west, this influence must carry into the collapsed model. We define the $reach_{NS}$ of the template as the absolute value of farthest distance of an influenced cell from the reference cell in the north-south direction and the $reach_{EW}$ of the template as the analogous parameter in the east-west direction. These parameters are illustrated in Figure 3-3.

Specification of Rules. Up to now, we have not given very much attention to the nature of the transition function (or rules). But, as a first approximation, we

---

[b]The original templates may have "holes"; if the "holes" coincide, they carry over to the template for the collapsed model.

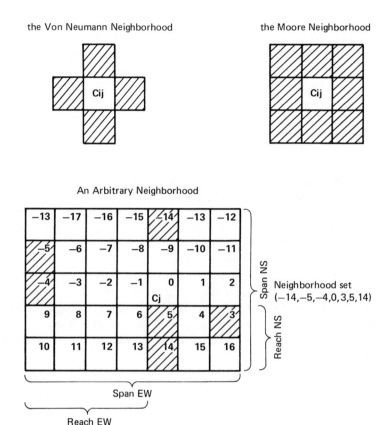

Figure 3-3. Definition and Characteristics of the Neighborhood Set.

can see that the number of rules need not exceed thnumber of states, where a rule consists of a statement of the following sort: "cell$_{ij}$ assumes state k if R_k obtains." Rules, however, may be complex themselves. Thus R_K could be a statement of the form:

$$R_K = (A_1) \cdot L \cdot (A_2) \cdot L \cdot (A_3) \dots L \cdot (A_M)$$

where $A_1, A_2, \dots, A_M$ are conditions applying to neighborhoods $N_1, N_2, \dots, N_M$ and $\cdot L \cdot$ is some logical operator. (Thus, a rule could be thought of as a string of FORTRAN logical IF statements.) The complexity of the individual rules R_k can be examined from a number of different viewpoints. Let it suffice for the moment that the effect of lengthening a rule by the element $\cdot L \cdot A_{m+1}$ can be measured in terms of the additional computer time needed to complete the computation of R_k over a standard configuration.[c]

In brief, the statement of rules as in the representational models of Chapter 2 can be translated into a lamination-by-lamination formalization of one rule per state [for example, $m_1, m_2, \ldots$ rules, where each individual rule has attached to it a numerical (computer-time) index]. In the collapse of laminations, the number of rules and their complexity indices are unchanged except that they now determine the transformed-state indices. The number of rules in the collapsed model equals Σ_m, the number of rules in the original laminar model.

Remarks: The collapse of laminations may be looked at intuitively in the following manner. Suppose there were a region in which a society carried on its demographic life on the surface of the earth while underneath the earth's surface a mining industry was operated by another society. Each society operates without knowledge of the other, and there are no mutual interactions. The two societies could be modeled separately, or a single record could be kept of their activity according to map coordinates. [For example, in sector (North 37, West 21) a child was born, while under the surface of the earth 3 tons of ore were extracted. The birth might have an impact in some 25 cells adjoining (N37,W21). These impacts could be calculated ignoring what goes on under the ground. But this brings us to the next step in the theorem—consideration of cross-laminar relationships.]

Case 2

A model that contains intralaminar relationships as in Case 1 and also contains cross-laminar relationships which do not increase the number of cell states, can be simply collapsed.

Step 1. Ignore all cross-laminar relationships and collapse the model as in Case 1. For $m_1, m_2 \ldots, m_j$ original states, there will be M_j states in the collapsed model (calculated as before), and the transformed neighborhood will have parameters $REACH_N$ and $REACH_W$. (See Figure 3-3.)

Step 2. Consider the cross-laminar relationships one by one. Each relationship will have a neighborhood template which originally applied to a designated lamination(s). This template can be applied now to the collapsed cellular space.

[c]R_k forms a finite group over the permutations of N_M; this allows one to place an upper limit on the computer time needed to calculate transitions for the most elaborate model possible. The approximation of R_k by computer time, as in the text, may lead to some overstatement of rule complexity if the original conditions were crudely and redundantly stated.

Since the cell states associated with a particular lamination can be identified, the transition rule can be applied (simulated) without ambiguity. No new cell states are created (by definition). The neighborhood may or may not be increased in size; again the templates are superimposed, and the new neighborhood template for the collapsed system will be the outer boundary of overlaid templates. The number of rules does not increase above the sum of states in individual laminations, but the complexity indices of the rules increase by the additional steps, $\cdot L \cdot A(m + \lambda)$, needed to calculate λ cross-laminar relationships.

Remarks. In terms of the example of the surface versus the mining societies, Case 2 allows states underground to influence states above ground, and vice versa. [For example, mining noise puts the child into a distressed state. People in parental states are excused from the labor force (above or below ground).] As in the examples of Chapters 1 and 2, the crossing of laminations opens up the model to a rich variety of behavior. What is significant to note, however, is that on a first and crude impression, the apparent complexity of the system is not as much influenced by the fact of cross-laminar relationships as by the more basic fact of distinct laminations (or, classifications of cell types). One also notes from Cases 1 and 2 that the collapse of laminations could take place in any order and in any direction, as the processes which define the number of cell states (the number of rules and the neighborhood template of the collapsed model) are unaffected by the order of reductions. As a corollary, we note that the direction of rules in a laminar model is immaterial; e.g., rules going up from the population plane to capital or down from capital to the population plane are equivalent in the reduced model.[d]

Case 3

A model is identical to that of Case 2 but also contains an additional μ conditions (cell states) which are determined only by cross-laminar relationships. The model collapses to a UCS, as in Cases 1 and 2. Neighborhoods are again determined by the overlay of templates, and state expansion will be no greater than $2^{\mu}M$, where M is the number of states in the prior model.

This case is shown quite simply. Model each additional condition as a distinct cellular space (lamination). Now reduce the model as in Case 2. Template overlay will determine the final neighborhood. By Equation (3.1), each reduction of a lamination will result in a doubling of the number of cell states for the prior model. Thus μ repetitions lead to a maximum expansion to $2^{\mu}M$ states. Particular models may permit several conditions to operate on a single lamination, and so the total expansion may be less.

---

[d]The reason to distinguish the direction of rule effects is that in a hierarchic laminar model with boundary conditions the convention of a primary direction is intuitive and also serves as a good method of avoiding programming errors (and overshooting boundaries).

Summary and Evaluation of Theorem 3-1. By the collapsing moves described by Cases 1, 2, and 3, any uniform laminar model can be reduced to a two-dimensional uniform cellular space. The reduction results in the following: expansion of cell states (index parameter, m'); a normalization of rules to the form of (FORTRAN) logical statements (the complexity characteristic of such statements can be indexed in a number of ways, but f', the computing time needed to execute the rules for a reference configuration, is a practical measure); reduction of all neighborhoods to a single neighborhood, accomplished by the method of successive overlays. (Useful parameters with which to describe the neighborhood are R^N and R^W, which give the reach from the reference cell, and X^N and X^W, which give the overall dimensions of span of the minimal prism, e.g., enclosing rectangle, for the template.)

In brief, any working representational SUR model in ULHCS form can be reduced to an image UCS and described by a relatively small number of complexity indices. These indices are readily computable; in fact, the indices may be decomposed to show the proportions of a particular index that are associated with boundary conditions, with the complexity of a particular component, or with a variety of other conditions. A numerical example of the reduction of a ULHCS and calculations based on Theorem 3-1 are given in Appendix 3A, but for the moment we should consider some direct uses of Theorem 3-1.

Economic Applications. Let us say we are working with a model Y_0 with image UCS Y'_0 and complexity parameters $\vec{P}'_0$. Typical model variations might be the alteration of a particular rule leading to model Y_1, the extension of the range of a particular interaction leading to model Y_2, lengthening of a production sequence (adding a lamination) leading to model Y_3, and so forth. Operating by brute force, one could produce $(Y'_1, \vec{P}'_1)$, $(Y'_2, \vec{P}'_2)$, ... However, in many instances it will be possible to calculate the incremental effect of a particular variation on an element of $\vec{P}$ directly, and in many instances one could operate with a partially collapsed basic model. Statements such as the following are reasonable and practicable: (1) Adding a particular interaction to the model increases a state-complexity measure by 20 percent and increases the reach of the image template by 50 percent in both directions. (2) A particular technical change results in no expansion of neighborhood size since it utilizes existing interactions. (3) Lengthening of a production chain leads to an order-of-magnitude increase in state complexity with no increase in the neighborhood template or rule complexity.

These statements may have significant underlying economic meaning. For example, it may be possible to associate statement (1) with a requirement of a 20 percent increase in the number of machines needed to handle the increased burden of communications, and a 50 percent increase in the number of long hauls, over the transportation system. Statement (2) could associate with a pure, disembodied, neutral change that requires no accommodating infrastructure. Statement (3) suggests a technical change which requires a heavy loading of low-range and middle-range administrators to handle implementation and management.

The theorem has significant heuristic applications as well. For example, the demographic models of Chapter 2 specified the "extended family" or "household" as the basic unit of analysis with individuals represented as state characteristics of the household. However, it would have been equally reasonable to have based the model on "individuals" with "families" forming an association on a higher lamination. One could compare complexity measures for models based on the separate approaches to obtain information on the modeling process itself. The "family" basis gives rise to a large state index but a low level of interactions. The "individuals" basis gives rise to units with low (modeled) complexity indices but which enter a system with a high measure of interactive complexity. Discrepancies between overall complexity measures (as defined in the following section) would suggest omissions (intentional or otherwise) in what is captured in the representation and would guide its development. Theorem 3-1 also guides one in the construction of large-scale models. It is possible to collapse several laminations into one and then similate the behavior of the reduced lamination by a simpler system that captures its essential characteristics. Using this format, one could build detail on higher laminations and the system as a whole while maintaining linkages to the suppressed sector. This procedure is followed in Chapter 6, which develops a "parable" of industrial development in terms of abstract cellular units, each of which represents an automaton simulating a highly complex socioeconomic system which is independently representable as a multilaminar cellular space. The potentialities for sectoral decomposition (preserving system characteristics) are unlimited.

Complexity Trade-offs

We have established that a ULHCS can be reduced to a UCS and that information obtained in the reduction can, of itself, be valuable in complexity analysis. But suppose we have two distinct ULHCS models or model variants, where one represents a condition in Japan, the other a condition in France; or one represents a condition in France in 1970, the other a condition in France in 1870; or one represents France as portrayed by one model-builder, the other by another model-builder. In each of these pairwise comparisons, the ULHCS models can be reduced to their image UCS models and associated parameters. The questions now are whether and how these UCS images can be compared. What we show in this section is that any UCS can be transformed into a UCS of standard type. The complexity parameters of the standardized UCS become the basis for comparison, and by means of a sequence of computable steps one can normalize further and derive a unique scalar measure of system complexity. The steps involved in such reductions are given by Theorems 3-2, 3-3, and 3-4 and associated corollary statements and definitions. The theorems were first developed by Smith (1971a, 1971b). They are paraphrased for the present application and presented without proof but with brief explanations.

To recapitulate, a UCS can be described by a cardinal index S which gives the number of states assumed by each cell for the state set V; cardinal indices $\vec{N}$ for the set N of cells comprising the cell neighborhood[e]; the dimensionality of the cellular space [e.g., the space is described as one-, two- (as here), or d-dimensional] ; and a factor T which represents the time needed to compute an iteration of the transition function f operating over an arbitrary region of the cellular space as compared with the time needed to calculate a transition f' for some reference UCS. Full comparability requires that f' operates over a configuration (CONF) that f would apply to. To generalize we define as the basis for simulations the global transition function F and the relevant domain of configurations CONF.

Definition: *A Global Transition Function* F: CONF $\rightarrow$ CONF is defined recursively: $F^t(\text{conf}) = F\left[F^{t-1}(\text{conf})\right]$. The set of global transition functions is labeled ϕ_d for d-dimensional space.

Definition: Z_1 and Z_2 are different d-dimensional cellular spaces. CONF_1, CONF_2, F_1, and F_2 are, respectively, configurations and global transition functions. τ_1 and τ_2 are positive integers, and we say that Z_2 *simulates* Z_1 with time factor $T = \tau_2/\tau_1$. If $T = 1$, the simulation occurs in *real time*; if $T > 1$, there is a *slow down* of time. If $T < 1$, there is a *speed up*. The simulation is valid *iff* $\exists$ a mapping G: $\text{CONF}_1 \rightarrow \text{CONF}_2$ and parallel time sequence g: $\phi \rightarrow \phi$ such that $F_2 = g(F_1)$. That is:

$$F_2 \left[G(\text{conf}) \right] = G \left[F_1 (\text{conf}) \right]$$

but requiring, respectively, τ_1 and τ_2.

Remarks: These highly general conditions obtain in a UCS derived from a representational ULHCS.

THEOREM 3-2. A cellular space Z with an arbitrarily (large) neighborhood can be reduced to a cellular space Z' with the von Neumann neighborhood (in two dimensions). There is a slowdown of computation which is proportional to neighborhood reach.

Specifically,

---

[e]A separate characteristic is the compactness and connectivity of the neighborhood template for given N.

$$T = \sum_{j=0}^{d-1} \text{reach}_j$$

where reach j is defined as the longest distance from the reference cell of a template to the wall of the minimum prism enclosing the template (moving in the direction of the jth dimension). Reach$_j$ is illustrated in the Figure 3-3. (Note: It is interesting that the slowdown is proportionate to the longest reach of the neighborhood, and not to its cardinal index.)

There is, in addition, an increase in cell states. For r original states, the cell states increase to s, and the increase will depend upon the full span of the enclosing prism. The state expansion is defined recursively. For i indexing dimensions, we begin

$s_{-1} = r$

$s_0 = r(r+1)^{w_{d-1}}$, w_{d-1} defined as the span of prism in dimension $d-1$

$s_i = s_{i-1} \cdot (s_{i-1} + 1)^{w_d - (i+1)}$

So that $s = s_d = s_{d-1} \cdot (s_{d-2} + 1)^{-2}$.

This theorem is proved by Smith (1971a, Section 3.1) by showing that the smaller von Neumann neighborhood template can "step out" to the full reach of the original neighborhood, but that this naturally requires additional time and an expansion of cell states to program the movements. In effect, the von Neumann template resets cell states in its immediate neighborhood and then slides over these intervening cells, taking rook moves. Its next movement and setting of states are determined by the preparatory step. Movements must cover the entire span of the neighborhood prism, so that this fact determines state expansion. What this theorem shows is that any UCS can be expressed parametrically in terms of a reference UCS, in this case the von Neumann automaton. It follows that any two arbitrary UCS models can be compared in terms of their von Neumann parameters.

There are, however, other possible bases for comparison, and Smith prepares a body of theorems by which one can establish "simulating equivalency" and therefore inferential complexity comparisons. These are paraphrased below.

THEOREM 3-3. An arbitrary d-dimensional cellular space can be simulated by d-dimensional cellular space with the Moore template (and an arbitrary Moore automaton can be simulated by a von Neumann automaton). Simulating parameters can be calculated (Smith, Sections 3.6, 3.7).

Theorems 3-2 and 3-3 involve the equivalence of [automata with small cells (low-state indices) and large neighborhoods] and [simulating automata with large cells and small neighborhoods]. Theorem 3-4 describes the reverse simulation equivalence: that between [large cells with small neighborhoods] and [simulating automata with a small (two-state) cell and large neighborhoods].

THEOREM 3-4. An arbitrary d-*dimensional* r-*state, von Neumann cellular space can be simulated by a* d-*dimensional, two-state automaton in real time but where the neighborhood index is expanded to* N' *a function of* r *and* d. T' *is bounded and computable (Smith, Section 1.2).*

Theorem 3-5 treats the final trade-off, that between complexity and simulating time. These theorems (3-3 to 3-5) are proved by Smith using constructions similar to those used here for Theorem 3-1. However, they involve additional notations that do not add any economic insights. A current area of research involves the reduction of ULHCS models to various reference UCS forms. When a particular UCS with significant intuitive attractions is found, the theorems will be translated accordingly.

THEOREM 3-5. An arbitrary r-*state* d-*dimensional cellular space can be simulated by a von Neumann automaton in* $1/k$ *times real time,* k *arbitrary.*[f]

Remarks: This body of theorems permits comparison of automata on a consistent basis. To show how they might be applied, consider the following sample analysis. Two economic systems differ in the "roundaboutness" of production. The systems are represented in ULHCS form by models Y and Y' in (respectively) L and $L + 1$ laminations (e.g., a tool-lathe sequence versus a tool-lathe-machine sequence). We suppose, for the sake of the analysis, that the first L laminations in M' are identical to those in M. The differences between M and M' will then be associated with neighborhood relationships and cell size (state index) in the $(L + 1)$st lamination and below. Y and Y' are composed of automata in two-dimensional laminations, and each system can be reduced to Z and Z' in two-dimensional UCS form. These reductions, of course, will generate extremely complicated neighborhood relationships and large state spaces. In practice, Y and Y' and Z and Z' will not be directly comparable; however, by Theorem 3-2 we can calculate two-parameter measures $(P_0, P_1), (P'_0, P'_1)$ for simulating von Neumann automata, by Theorem 3-5 we can produce one-parameter measures s, s' for real-time simulating von Neumann automata, and by Theorem 3-3 we can produce alternate one-parameter measures s_m, s'_m for simulating Moore automata.

The preceding example represents the resolution of a case proposed in the discussion of Theorem 3-1. But note we had no need to restrict ourselves to models which differ only in a single characteristic. The single-parameter

[f]Understandably, state expansion is above that of an ordinary simulation, and it is not yet clear how the bounding of a configuration affects this result.

complexity measures could have been derived for arbitrary UCS models (e.g., for arbitrary reference ULHCS models), and the comparison would stand. It should be understood, of course, that the derivation of a scalar complexity index may not be the procedure of choice in a particular application and that one may prefer to operate with some other reduction of the model or some particular constellation of parameters. One may also wish to make more of rule complexity than was done here[g]; these are matters of style, choice, convenience, and purpose in a specific application. What we have done was demonstrate reduction and standardization potentialities; we can wait for experience to demonstrate which of these potentialities is most useful.

Appraisal of the Technique

There are still a number of matters that have to be considered in an evaluation of these procedures. These are given in brief outline form.

(1) There is not yet a body of experience to indicate the relative advantages of any one simulating automaton or parameter measure over another. Development of acceptable indices of complexity is accordingly an empirical and judgmental matter.

(2) The relationship between computer time and complexity measures requires particular elaboration. In practice, one may compare models, Y and Y' without actually transforming them into simulating automata. In this case, the equivalence theorems would be used to find out whether to associate complexity differences with cell-state or with neighborhood complexity. The quantification of complexity might involve comparisons of actual computing times, using the theorems to "explain" what is observed. This brings out pragmatic problems. The complexity trade-off measures give upper limits for computing time in specific simulating automata; a computer program is itself a simulating automaton, but its relationship to the comparison automata will depend upon program efficiency. For example, redundant DO loops or DO loops with too large a range would lead to an overstatement of required time. Programmer choice is thus an element, as is computer or algorithm efficiency.

(3) However, there is an important aspect to bring out on this matter of subjectivity. As noted in the discussion of Theorem 3-1, complexity measures should not be affected by different approaches to sectoralization or laminar organization; so, to this extent, the technique is "experimenter-proof." In contrast, differences in drawing sectoral lines in standard econometric models produce order-of-magnitude effects in system computability characteristics.

(4) The question of the appropriate dimension for the simulating automata has been left open. A hierarchic system composed of two-dimensional lamina-

---

[g]Again, rule complexity has been ignored in this section. As in the construction of Theorem 3-1, rule complexity can be handled via a simple measure of required computer time.

tions can be reduced to a large two-dimensional UCS. However, it may also be susceptible to translation into a three-dimensional structure of simulating automata. The operating characteristics of simulating three-dimensional automata are in practice unknown—but, of course, the theorems apply.

(5) The reader may worry that we have ignored dynamic considerations by focusing almost entirely on structural aspects. We note that the CA model is intrinsically dynamic and lends itself to the tracking of complexity in dialectic sequences such as the movement to more roundabout production or other developmental processes.

(6) An economic model can also be specified in terms of "slow automata" which impose delays on particular interactions, e.g., communications or transportation in the ULHCS model. A UCS can simulate a slow-automata system and show the effects of the lag structure in its real-time behavior.

(7) Most of the structural results examined here also apply to "stochastic automata," which express state transitions probabilistically.

Appendix 3A:
Numerical Calculation of
Complexity Parameters

The numerical example developed in this Appendix shows how complexity-measurement theory may be applied. By necessity a contrived example is given. We assume two technologies, each of which produces an identical final product. Model 1 represents a primitive technology consisting of a simple three-worker shop where handtools made by the workers themselves are employed. Model 2 represents a roundabout technology. The same sort of three-worker shop is used except that each shop builds one of four components and the final product is put together in an assembly stage. We think of the stages as laminations and describe the models accordingly. The lowest lamination consists of a socioeconomic demographic plane, which we need not consider in detail, since for convenience it is assumed to be unaffected by the technology in use. Lamination 1 gives the distribution of workers free to work on production. Lamination 2 gives "workshops," and lamination 3 gives the assembly operation in model 2.

Model 1

Now let us consider model 1 in some detail. For the first lamination we specify two states: (1) presence of a worker (surplus relative to activities on lamination 0), and (2) "not employed by another shop." For convenience we restrict the neighborhood of "worker" cells to the cell itself. On the second lamination we specify the workshop by: an "on" state which depends on the presence of three workers and three tools and the absence of an encroaching workshop; by four "tool states" corresponding to vintages of tools; and by eight production levels based on an arbitrary integer function of tool states in the preceding period and a predetermined replacement policy for tools. The production schedule can be made much fancier, but only a simple construction is needed here.

Each workshop has a neighborhood of 3-by-3 cells on the second lamination governing encroachment by other workshops (this is a programming convention) and a neighborhood of 4-by-4 cells on the first lamination from which to draw workers. The rules (and again these are an arbitrary set of conditions) consist of (1) a three-step rule controlling the "on" switch; (2) a four-step aging function; and (3) an eight-step production schedule.

These conditions are summarized in Table 3A-1 in a format that allows easy calculation according to Theorem 3-1.

Stage 1: By Theorem 3-1 (Case 1) we collapse the model according to own-lamination states. The resulting simulation model will have the following parameters.

Table 3A-1
Model 1: Summary of Model Characteristics

Field	States on Own Lamination	M	Cross-laminar States	Neighborhood		Rule Index	M_i'
				Maximum	Reach		
Lamination 2	One "on" switch	13	Two worker states	4 by 4	2 by 2	10x(1 step)	
	Eight production levels					1x(3 step)	
	Four tool states					1x(4 step)	
						1x(8 step)	
							25
Cross-lamination				3 by 3			
Lamination 1	Two worker states	2		1 by 1		1x(2 step)	
							2

State parameter $= M_2 = 1 + m_1 + m_1 m_2 = 1 + 2 + 13 + 26 = 42$ states

Neighborhood parameter = a 4-by-4 maximum neighborhood with 2-by-2 reach

Time factor $= 1 + m'_1 + m'_2 + m'_1 m'_2 = 1 + 2 + 25 + 50 = 78$ computer units

The calculation of state and neighborhood parameters is straightforward. However, the calculation of the computer-time index is entirely arbitrary and is based on a working assumption that one two-step rule is equivalent to two one-step rules. The final columns of the table give working figures for the time indices which are then combined according to Theorem 3-1. The figure of 78 units represents a *maximum* figure since "efficient" programming might be able to reduce the number of required computation steps. The units themselves are undimensioned. It would take inferences based on empirical analysis to attach real-world referents to this index—and, for that matter, to the other indices.

Stage 2: By Theorem 3-1, Case 2, in the second stage of collapsing the system, the state and neighborhood indices remain the same, but the computer-time index increases but to no more than 130 units. Since Case 3 does not apply, we have as our final parameters a 42-state automata over a 4-by-4 neighborhood with 2-by-2 reach. The computer-time index is given as 130 unspecified units.

Model 2

Model 2 differs from model 1 in the following respects: 1 additional worker-state is distinguished corresponding to "organizational-administrative talent." This arbitrary embellishment increases cell states on the first lamination to three. On lamination 2 we require four additional states to distinguish the different types of workshop. We also add four rule steps to distinguish shops and eight rule steps to govern the on switch according to states in other shops. The summary parameters for laminations 1 and 2 before considering lamination 3 are given in Table 3A-2.

If we calculate as before, the collapsed model has the previous neighborhood, 104 cell states $(1 + 3 + 25 + 75)$ and a computer-time index not exceeding 184 units $(1 + 3 + 45 + 135)$.

The Assembly Stages. Adding the third lamination for an assembly facility requires by assumption a larger neighborhood corresponding to a transportation system that allows communication betweeen the assembly plant and at least one of the shops. We stipulate a 12-by-4 "road" which leads to a maximum neighborhood of 12-by-4 (the road is arbitrarily oriented so as to have a 10-by-2 reach).

To keep state complexity within bounds, we specify only four final output

Table 3A-2
Model 2: Summary of Characteristics of Laminations 1 and 2

| Field | States on Own Lamination | M | Cross-laminar States | Neighborhood | | Rule Index | M' |
				Maximum	Reach		
Lamination 2	13 states from model 1 plus 4 shop states 8 "on" switches	25		4 by 4	2 by 2	25 states and 20 additional steps	45
Cross-lamination			Two worker states	3 by 3			
Lamination 1	Three worker states	3		1 by 1			3

states based on workshop outputs. These are cross-laminar relationships to be considered subsequently, but we also specify an own-lamination, two-state, "on" switch based on the presence for two periods of an "administrator." The tabulation based on own-lamination parameters and Cases 1 and 2 of Theorem 3-1 leads to $M = 1 + 2 + 104 + 208 = 315$. In addition, we obtain a 12-by-4 neighborhood with 10-by-2 reach. On parallel calculations we obtain time factor $M' = 1 + 2 + 184 + 368 = 555$. Again, these are the parameters for lamination 3 collapsed onto laminations 1 and 2 without considering the cross-laminar relationships.

Cross-laminar Relationships. To account for the exclusive cross-laminar relationships by Case 3 the state and computer-time indices must be expanded by a factor of 2^μ where μ is the number of exclusive cross-laminar states. In the example $\mu = 4$, so the states and the indices would increase by a factor of 16. On this calculation we obtain $2^\mu \times 135 = 16 \times 135 = 5040$ states and a time factor of $16 \times 555 = 8080$.

To illustrate heuristic experimentation we now introduce model 2 in which we "discover" an organization efficiency that reduces μ to unity (an "on" switch) but at the cost of additional state complexity on lamination 2. Without this efficiency, the state and computer-time indices would expand enormously; with it, an enormous qualitative complexity reduction occurs. This is fanciful, but the analysis points to a critical area in which technical change may be induced.

In summary, the impact of increased roundaboutness is expressed in the final table of parameters for models 1, 2, and 2a. The figures for model 2a are again approximate based on a contrived technical change.

	μ	States	Neighborhood	Reach	Computer time
Model 1		42	4 by 4	2 by 2	130
Model 2	4	5,040	12 by 4	10 by 2	8080
Model 2a	1	$\approx 1,000$	12 by 4	10 by 2	≈ 1500

Comments

The example is naive to an embarrassing degree: the figures used are quite artificial, no general-equilibrium conditions have been entered, and the model is stingy with controls. (Model 2 lacks feedback and optimizing controls and is subject to grotesque "bang-bang" behavior.) However, standard market or planning adoptive mechanisms would change the complexity parameters only slightly, and the figures here seem typical and representative of patterns that could emerge in shifts toward roundaboutness. We again note that the first step of roundaboutness seems to call forth the most profound effects in required complexity. Where the first step seems to imply a double order-of-magnitude increase in the measures, the second step seems to require an order-of-magnitude increase and subsequent steps significantly less. Even when we recognize that these are tentative results obtained in arbitrary and stylized models, the analysis nevertheless seems highly suggestive on a number of problems in development and capital theory.

We note finally that calculations were carried only up to the point of applying the trade-off theorems. Experience with the method is needed before we can make an intelligent choice of benchmark automata, and it seemed reasonable to limit the complexity reduction to four parameter indices, which should be suggestive individually of infrastructural conditions.

4 Technical Change

It is obvious that we are at the very early and experimental stages of developing the concept of complexity in a systematic fashion. This chapter will, in effect, propose an agenda for such analysis. The first step will be taxonomic, relating complexity to classifications of technical change that seem to have some promise as analytical categories. This tentative characterization attempts to identify aspects of the complexity dimension which will illuminate at least some of the following viewpoints on the economics of production technology and technical change.

1. One well-known view is that "specialization" (in the Adam Smith sense) leads to an increase in system complexity and organization. Many technical changes are of this sort, but the complexity dimension is frequently lost alongside the immediate measurement of input—output productivity. The attempt here will be to develop measures that would emerge as computable adjuncts to conventional productivity measurement.
2. The development view is that organizational specialization frequently has an infrastructural cost—particularly where the complexity interactions relate to communications requirements or market exchanges. The attempt here will be to develop complexity concepts that could be used in applied analysis of the "absorption" question.
3. A corollary view states that preexistence of infrastructural elements encourages expansion of matching complex and specialized processes. The relevant applied contexts are the study of urban structures (as in Jacobs), the study of avenues for the diffusion of technical change, and central-place theory.
4. The systems view recognizes the direct productivity advantages of specialization but considers the aggregative dynamic behavior of organized interacting components. In particular, this view focuses on the failure potential of complex systems which arises either from the breakdown of vital sectors (the teamster theory of bargaining) or from the dead weight of the organizational burden.[a]
5. One important contemporary view involves ecological concern with the encroachment of the byproducts of technology on the environment. The interest here will be on identifying the incidence of external effects of technical change within a complex system.

---

[a]This is a recurrent theme in speculative fiction. Among the most gripping images in modern literature is Isaac Asimov's description in the *Foundation* trilogy of the fall and decay of the imperial planet Trantor. Gibbon has something to say on these matters as well.

It should be noted that in inspecting the complexity aspect of technology the discussion can move along some conjectural and speculative avenues. Two such avenues are given at this point:

6. A developmental view which relates classes of technology to the spatial organization of social units is one avenue. A more or less conventional question within this category concerns the relative efficiency of a particular production technique in particular spatial situations, i.e., where population is organized as in an Indian peasant village versus a small city. But one could move toward utopian conjectures as to the feasibility of commune or cottage-industry organization of large sectors of society. All these conjectures touch on the social and demographic structures which, in association with predecessor technologies, led to current spatial patterns.
7. Another avenue lies in a related planning viewpoint, which is concerned with the possibility of influencing technological development so as to encourage particular social and spatial configurations.

On this motivation, we propose to develop terminology and definitions that will distinguish technical changes with significant external, environmental, or developmental effects.

Let us take as our beginning point a representational model, Y_0, of a particular socioeconomic system. A technological change occurs (or is projected), and its outcome is represented by the (reprogrammed) model Y_1. Following the logic of the preceding chapter, we specify for Y_0 and Y_1 simulating automata, Z_0 and Z_1; and for these forms we calculate the sets of complexity parameters P_{0i} and P_{1i}. We would expect that a change that merits consideration would lead to "improvements" in a number of standard measures of physical productivity, but that a change which alters the complexity parameters poses the prospect of significant qualitative change. Thus, for example, we would expect the complexity indices to distinguish between a case of "simple learning" as a source of productivity increase and such dramatic cases as the "green revolution" or "the installation of the factory system." But we would hardly need an elaborate analytical apparatus for this; the issue becomes interesting, however, if a complex of changes affects the system at a given time. Some will apparently increase complexity (e.g., increases in roundaboutness of production that increase the number of links or putative transactions). However, the apparent system complexity increase may be offset by changes in component complexity (e.g., the new development may double existing interactions or abolish others). In short, the direction and extent of the change in complexity may confuse and defeat assessment by intuition alone.

As a first attempt at resolving these matters, we suggest the following terminology.

Technical change is *parametric* if on adjustment to equilibrium the complexity indices in an appropriate automata representation remain unchanged (to a reasonable approximation). Technical change is *nonparametric* if there is significant change in the complexity parameters.

Nonparametric changes may be identified with *component complexity* or with *organizational complexity*. In the latter case, the change may be associated with either (or both) extension of the span of organization (e.g., horizontal broadening of neighborhoods) or with lengthening of the production process (e.g., vertical roundaboutness).

Parametric Change

To develop the taxonomy, let us consider the range of behaviors possible under parametric change, a variation in production that does not alter the complexity measures. This should be the least ambiguous variety and the one that comes closest to the stereotype of technical change in equilibrium capital and growth theory. However, as we will see, pure parametric change turns out to be an unlikely eventuality.

Figure 4-1 gives a portrayal of a field for such change. We have a hierarchic

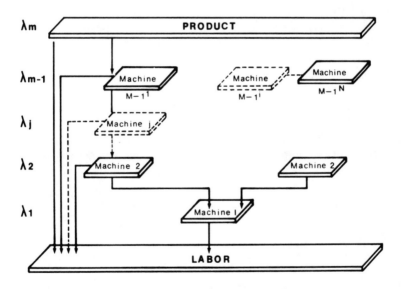

Figure 4-1. Roundabout Processes

process on m machine laminations where each lamination represents a distinct type of machine which is used to make a machine on a higher lamination. The λ_j are production coefficients with the following definition:

$$\lambda_j = \lambda'_j L_j$$

where λ'_j is output per worker employed on the machine and L_j is a labor requirement. Assuming a strict technology (e.g., fixed proportions, λ'_j and L_j are measures associated with full machine capacity. We allow machines to be operated at full capacity or shut down entirely.[b]

We label the diagramed entity a *production configuration, CONF*, and at this time distinguish only the *active state* in which a component is operated at its full capacity.[c] The production system is defined to be *in equilibrium* if, with respect to the active state, $\text{CONF}_t = \text{CONF}_0$ for all t in T, the time span of interest.[d] If we limit ourselves for the moment to equilibrium sequences, we note the following economic characteristics of the model.

1. The model has neo-Austrian coloration in its precise enumeration of the stages of production.
2. There are no capital-measurement problems; any component in the system (including labor) could be taken as the basis for ratio calculations (within this subsystem in the equilibrium state).
3. The model fits several conventional sectoralization schemes—for example, by collapsing laminations $m - 1$ through 1, we form a capital-goods sector as a simple UCS. We could form a one-sector model by further collapsing the mth sector on the capital UCS.

Technical Change

Now let us examine what might be meant by "parametric technical change" for the system. Let us say the change has the effect of changing the ratio of outputs to the labor input. We say that prior to the change there was an output of Q

---

[b]These are simply assumptions of convenience. If one's tastes ran in such a direction, one could also specify full neoclassical substitutability in a representation at little cost in computer time. For simple numerical examples, one could normalize "machines" so that $L_j = 1$ for all j.

[c]We have no need to consider the problem (which is trivial in this context) of specifying the replacement conditions for each component. The next footnote treats the dynamics of configurations where components are subject to aging.

[d]The definition permits us to describe T, for example, as every Kth observation, in which case we include under the definition of "equilibrium" a case in which a reference configuration reappears periodically—the interim periods allowing the drawing down and replacement of intermediate capital. The specification of technical coefficients is most convenient if we assume a "one-horse shay" component that operates without deterioration up to the point of its instantaneous decay and replacement.

physical units. After the change, but maintaining $CONF_0$ (that is, after the change but prior to a system adjustment), output is $Q_1 = Q_0(1 + \phi)$, $\phi > 0$. Let us ask if there are any reasonable (or standard) economic assumptions that will preserve the original equilibrium configuration, that is, maintain $CONF_0 = CONF_1 = CONF_t$. If so, these assumptions become sufficient conditions for parametric change.

One special case meets sufficiency, another comes close; from these we will derive general or necessary conditions. The special case is one in which worker productivity increases but $CONF_0$ is preserved. The construction for the neoclassical model given in Figure 4-2 can be used to show the economic conditions underlying the case.[e] The axes give k, capital per worker (measured in m efficiency units) and y, output per worker. K_0 is the initial position, and π_0 is the initial rate of capital productivity. This is an equilibrium position, if π_0 is also equal to a "cost of capital" used to ration investment. That is, if this equality holds, there will be no inducement to deeper or shallow capital. A technical change is pictured in Figure 4-2a as an upward shift in the production curve. Now, $CONF_0$ is preserved if there is no alteration in the amount or structure of the capital good after all adjustments are worked through. Consider the pictured example: π_1, the post-change rate of capital productivity, is shown as equal to the prechange rate, but a problem still remains. Saving would ordinarily go up with increased income. For equilibrium to occur, we require some combination of the following special conditions: (1) A compensating shrinkage in the propensity to save;[f] (2) export of capital so that the capital market can clear with no increase in domestic investment; (3) a use of saving for

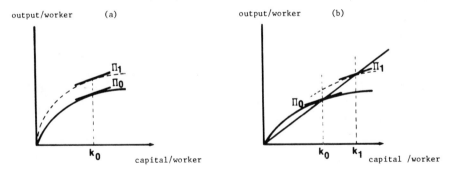

Figure 4-2. Technical Change in a Growth Process

---

[e]The neoclassical model can only be suggestive on this matter. Since the present model specifies heterogeneous capital, only a few steady-state results will transfer between the two formats. This point will be clarified subsequently.

[f]Such an adjustment in the saving propensity could be forced by various taxation policies but that would be contrary to the equilibrium or golden-age motif that we are currently investigating.

nonproductive expenditures such as palaces, cathedrals, etc.; (4) a use of saving in special sectors such as education or research and development that, in fact, contribute to the observed system growth (this mechanism is explained in Albin, 1970 and 1975); (5) a compensatory expansion of capital accumulation in other sectors. These are restrictive and perhaps unreasonable conditions, implying that the result hypothesized is narrow and specialized. Conditions resulting in equilibrium for π, $\pi \neq \pi_0$, are similarly restrictive on saving behavior.

However, let us assume for the sake of the argument that the appropriate conditions hold over the process as a whole. We can then investigate what effect this general condition might have over the components and stages of the process. Two conditions for change seem easy to establish at the abstract level, namely, (1) that the change could remain parametric if rates of capital productivity, π_{1k}, calculated at all laminations are equal to one another and equal to π_1 and π_0, and (2) that the change could remain parametric if the laminar structure of the process were rigidly fixed, so that there would be no possibility of altering the machine proportions within the process. (The technical change must, furthermore, be disembodied for even these effects to hold unambiguously.)

In short, purely parametric change for any major portion of the system requires a rather rigid set of restrictions. We could develop a parallel argument for Harrod-neutral change [illustrated as (2)], but we would face the cumbersome construct of measuring machine units and complexity indices per labor efficiency unit.[g] Even more rigid requirements on the nature of the induced capital expansion would be required, and we would still require the lamination-by-lamination equality of π_{1k}. Codifying all this, we have what could be labeled a working proposition:

> Technical change is most likely to be nonparametric in nature since the requirements for parametric change are unduly restrictive. Necessary conditions are lamination-by-lamination equality of π_0 and π_1. These conditions plus the constellation of bias factors noted earlier act as sufficient conditions. A more restrictive case and a special construction is needed to give parametric change in the Harrod-neutral case.

Nonparametric Change

With this excursion complete, we can move on to the apposite case of nonparametric change. The first point to note is that we are necessarily forced out of golden-age equilibrium; so there will be no excuse for persisting with the notion of an aggregate capital measure. From here on in, the discussion will be

[g]In Harrod-neutral change there is an induced expansion of the capital stock that preserves the ratio of output to capital input. This is illustrated by equality between π_0 and π_1, along a ray from the origin. Harrod-neutral change is an "analytical convenience" that permits equilibrium where there is a proportionate saving function.

couched in terms of specifically labeled machines and components. The issue now is to characterize the significantly different varieties of nonparametric change. First we consider variations associated with complexity measures and then turn to variations associated with locational factors. We note further that the earlier discussion associates particular complexity parameters with particular attributes, namely, neighborhood size with transportation and communications requirements, a large number of interlaminar relationships with organizational requirements, and so on. Clearly a change in the number of laminations, *laminar change*, would have the most profound effects of any type of nonparametric change, but we need not restrict ourselves to this extreme case.

Technical-change Assessments

The complexity measurement theorems of the preceding chapter establish that any hierarchic system will have associated with it complexity parameters (c_1, $c_2, \ldots, c_i$). In certain instances one may be content with single-parameter measurement, in which case we identify the scalar C^* as the complexity index of a model collapsed into the UCS format. As we argue that technical change is likely to be nonparametric, it follows that such change will be associated with measurable change in C^* and/or in some of c_i.

The additional complexity may or may not require additional (infrastructural) investment, and such investment may or may not be under the internal control of the decision unit. It would be premature to attempt definitive analysis of these matters, but a few cases can be defined which are suggestive for future heuristic and empirical representations and for further theoretical study.

Institutional Problems of Technological Change

Let us say that we can determine a few associations between complexity parameters and infrastructional requirements. For example, suppose a measure of component complexity associates with a level of vocational training for workers, a measure of layering with a communications requirement, and a measure of neighborhood range with a requirement on the transportation system. We can formulate these associations in a number of different ways, but all point toward the general problem of technical forecasting.

Technical Forecasting

Suppose that we stipulate as a working assumption that the new technique will replace the old. It is possible to "substitute" the rules of the new technology for those of the old, and to recalculate complexity parameters and implicit infrastructural requirements for a new sequence, producing the same output as before.

These figures would be the transient requirements for the system. However, we would reason on standard capital-theoretic grounds that the installation would be incomplete until explicit and social rates of return for the system as a whole and at each component lamination were brought into alignment with a cost of finance. The full adjustment could be approximated by appropriate simulations that use any of a number of standard formulations for investment-adjustment equations. By the very nature of the problem, it is impossible to predict in advance what the exact end-result will be; however, it is reasonable to expect a few qualitative patterns. One is that the first stages of adjustment are likely to work on and use up slack resources, activities, and personnel states in the larger system and in the supply markets. A complicated economy tends to have such slack in its various supply and service departments—particularly in infrastructural areas. However, in later stages of installation of the new technology or composition of techniques, slack is likely to be used up, and services which were, in effect, provided as an external benefit to the activity will have to be internalized or otherwise paid for. In other words, in the typical institutional setting, the enterprises that plan, design, and control the technique "the boxes in the block diagram" purchase the communications, transportation, and special personnel requirements "the connecting lines on the diagram" from outside agencies. The problem of coordination is apparent, and one would expect to see a misestimate (generally an underestimate) of infrastructural requirements. Furthermore, the misestimate is likely to become evident only after the key decisions on whether to adopt the technique have already been made. This effect is imprecise and is hardly susceptible to statement as a formal proposition, but the reasoning suggests that an economy with a high rate of nonparametric change will be prone to serious forecasting errors in infrastructural development.

The Problem of Relative Efficiency –
LDC Absorption Problems

A closely related problem concerns the ability of LDC economies to absorb technologies from advanced countries. It has long been argued that success in designing, installing, and maintaining capital equipment is surely due to the presence of infrastructural elements of the sort just mentioned. In the advanced economy, such resources develop with predecessor advanced technologies and are available (subject to misestimation risk) to newer technologies and economic organizations. Technologies are developed with this consideration in the design formula; hence, it is inevitable that a transplanted technique appears as ineffi-

cient. This notion generalizes and formalizes easily, and the following propositions are suggested for empirical testing.

1. A transplanted technique will appear as relatively inefficient in its new
   location unless appropriate adjustments in machine costs are made at each
   lamination of the process in an attempt to equate rates of return over the
   process.
2. This will necessarily alter complexity parameters and infrastructural requirements from what they were in the original configuration.
3. The difficulties in adjustment will almost certainly be greatest in an LDC
   where the lack of infrastructural elements is typically a serious constraint.
4. Adjustment will be easiest in the more advanced economies where the
   preexisting complexity implicit in many coexisting techniques and production sequences gives rise to infrastructural slack (at least in the short run).

This is a somewhat artificial way to make a conventional institutional
statement—that the advanced countries will have a relative advantage in adopting
technologies—and a theoretical corollary statement—that specific constellations
of infrastructural elements give rise to relative advantages in the adaptation to
specific technologies. The reason to make the statements, however, is that they
are in this instance given the promise of direct verification through analysis of
the accompanying SUR structures.

Conclusions

This chapter has presented a taxonomy of technical changes and a number of
preliminary conjectives on technological transfers. The purpose of the exercise
was again that of demonstrating possibilities and proposing methodology. There
is no way to bypass the actual task of technological assessment for specific
processes, but the methods proposed here promise clarifications in some of the
more difficult problem areas of development and planning for technological
transfer. It should also be noted that most of the constructs introduced in this
chapter in terms of associations with infrastructural elements could also be put
in terms that are explicitly locational; i.e.; the geographic distribution of
infrastructural slack. Explicit development of corresponding locational models is
an important line for further research, but one that is strongly empirical and
hence outside the scope of this book. We note, finally, that identification of
critical infrastructural elements is the first step in identifying critical strategic
sectors of a system and also the first step in identifying those sectors which
impede a utopian design.

Part III:
System Behaviors

Introduction to Part III

In this part of the book we will engage a number of conjectures which are outside the usual domain of economic inquiry and social science research. We believe these conjectures to be on appropriate and relevant matters—but on matters that have been outside discipline studies because of the lack of suitable formal languages and analytical structures in which they could be expressed. The reciprocal relationship of methodology to field of inquiry is well known, and this book is not the appropriate medium for a long recitation on the sociology of knowledge, on paradigms, or on pragmatics. It is certainly clear that the substance and the domain of economic theory have changed in response to new mathematical developments. One has only to examine the index of a standard undergraduate text in price theory to see the impact of the mathematical theory of games or optimal-control theory, to take two recent examples, on the sorts of problems which are incorporated within the discipline.

However, dangers are involved in drawing applications from one discipline and attempting to install them in another. The relationship of a mathematical model to the real world is to some extent a metaphorical one, and the main danger is essentially that of expanding the metaphor or analogy beyond its useful limits. We may now be approaching such limits. We have argued that cellular-automata models can be put into correspondence with real-world systems. And as a result of such a correspondence, useful results can be obtained in simulation studies, as suggested in Part I, or in production analysis and capital theory, as suggested in Part II. We now extend the metaphor and ask if broad styles of inquiry which are specific to cellular-automata theory can be translated or transferred meaningfully into the behavioral sciences.

Chapter 5 begins the exploration with an examination of two fundamental theorems within CA theory: the von Neumann *self-reproduction* theorem and Moore's *Garden of Eden* conjecture. The chapter explains the concepts involved and suggests metaphorical counterparts with planning theory and general-equilibrium theory. The materials are presented in highly abstract form. The chapter shows that there are economic problems which bear resemblance to those adduced by von Neumann and Moore in the context of abstract representations of computing machinery, but no attempt is made at direct calculation or application—nor is it known whether such applications would be feasible.

In Chapter 6 we consider an extension of heuristic uses of CA theory and present a "parable" of growth and development in which primitive CA elements are employed to illustrate processes of qualitative change analogous to those which occur over larger historical time scales. No specific results are presented. The purpose of the chapter is to illustrate the feasibility of particular styles of representation.

Chapter 7 represents an excursion into welfare theory and social choice theory that draws heavily on results in computibility theory and Gödel logic. This line follows from results in abstract automata theory which show correspondence between cellular automata and Turing machine automata, but it should be stressed that the analysis presented here is less "metaphorical" than that in Chapters 5 and 6. It appears that the form of the social-choice model is essentially that of a universal Turing machine, so that problems of Gödel logic must be confronted. It can be shown that a fairly large list of problems in welfare theory are subject to such difficulties, and that a substantial area of inquiry is involved. At this point we will confine analysis to a single problem involving social-choice mechanisms. Although highly abstract in form, the problem has direct political relevance and current application.

5 Planning Conjectures

As noted in the introduction to Part III, we are engaged now in a metaphorical exercise. We have seen in earlier chapters that a number of problem areas in economics and the other behavioral sciences may be illuminated by the application of automata reasoning. We ask at this time if results which are specific to automata theory give rise to new insights or new formulations in the social and economic domain.

The Self-reproduction Problem

To begin, we examine the root problem in von Neumann's research on cellular automata—concern with the construction of an abstract representation of a self-reproducing machine, particularly a machine with computing capacity. The theory originated with this problem, and it is a worthwhile exercise to extend the analogy to the economic domain.

Von Neumann's work on the problem of complexity and self-reproduction must be traced through fragmentary evidence in the form of lectures, asides in other works, and incomplete research notes. He was working actively on the problem at the time of his death, and it is clear that he had broken through to a solution although the work was clearly not in its intended final form. In any case, successors have been able to complete the problem as set originally by von Neumann and along lines proposed in his notes. Von Neumann (1966) represents such a completion and compilation under the editorial direction of Burks.

The incomplete notes and fragments give revealing insights into von Neumann's approach, method of progress, and style of analysis; and one can surmise that these personal touches might have been lost or edited out of the eventual formal printed copy, had he lived to produce final finished journal articles on the subject. These tones come out most strongly in Burks (1970). Several themes should be noted before we pass to the formalism. The first is that of empirical content and referents. Although von Neumann developed his analysis in terms of an abstract computing-constructing machine, he formed his concept of complexity in terms of the empirical world and drew his insights not just from physical and mechanical processes but also from observations of biological, linguistic, and social systems.

The second theme is that of the "complexity threshold" (which von Neumann saw as critical in biological systems). In effect, von Neumann saw the first stages of complication as leading to unreliability, instability, and leveraged volatility. An order-of-magnitude increase in parts and in richness of interactions among parts was required if an automaton (read: organism or system) was to achieve self-regulated and self-maintained reliability—let alone the capacity to reproduce itself. This perspective is perhaps commonplace now, when one observes that in the largest computers one can afford to allocate core and circuitry to the machine's housekeeping and maintenance (personal care and homeostasis).

The third major theme is a concern with detail and literal construction. Von Neumann's notes are filled with meticulous diagrams and descriptions of the ways in which the parts of his construct could function or control and be controlled. Thus, each of von Neumann's 29 automaton states corresponds to an engineering function (e.g., a rigid member, a communication channel, etc.) that is susceptible to precise definition, illustration, and specification. Obviously, the states are then codified as mathematical abstractions, but the referents are always in the foreground.[a] Von Neumann's proof of the self-reproduction conjecture was literally a matter of construction, a demonstration that an automaton had to reach a critical level of inherent complexity before self-reproduction would become possible. It is not a matter of number of components or size, but rather what each component can do and how the components are put together.[b]

These preliminaries should give some feeling for the analysis and the way in which it was developed; it is now useful to look at the self-reproduction problem in a formal way.

Mathematical Conditions for Cellular
Self-reproduction

A cellular configuration, a finite array of cells, is designated as c. c' (disjoint from c) is a *copy* of c, if there exists a translation of c' onto c such that every cell c_j' in c' has the same state as its counterpart c_j in c.

[a]The theme of literalness requires emphasis since the descriptions of complexity measures in the preceding chapters seem to point toward axiomatization and simplification of systems (i.e., the reduction of a 29-state automaton to a simulating automaton with few states, the reduction of a ULHCS to a UCS). Such reductions or compressions are significant primarily as a means of deriving consistent descriptive parameters or convenient mathematical forms. The study of abstract automata is a burgeoning mathematical field, but we believe von Neumann's concern with specification and empirical referents to be the line that is most likely to produce insights in social science applications.

[b]The proof is lengthy and elaborate; see Burks (1970), von Neumann (1966), and Codd for its exposition. It is worth noting von Neumann's false starts. One approach which he pursued seriously was of a device operating in a fluid bath in which floated many components and spare parts. The problem was to construct a program that would trigger the device to search for parts, assemble them in the correct location with the correct orientation, and then activate the new device (if and when the original device can determine that it had produced a valid replica of itself).

The configuration c is labeled as capable of self-reproduction if the following conditions can obtain. Start at time $t = 0$ with all nonquiescent cells forming a configuration which is a copy of c. Then c is capable of self-reproduction by time t—if at time $T' < T$, S_T (the set of all nonquiescent cells) contains at least two disjoint copies of c and if at time T'' ($T' < T'' < T$) $S_{T''}$ contains at least three copies of c, etc.[c]

The theorem states that self-reproduction in this sense is possible for a finite device or system that exceeds a critical complexity measure. This complexity level would approximate that of the largest computing machines (supported, inferentially, by the industrial system that produces its components). Obviously the critical complexity level is attained by living organisms.

Self-reproduction in Economic Systems

Now we should ask what the economic associations of self-reproduction might be. The analogy cannot be exact, but the suggestion is that something more than simple growth is involved here, say the ability to produce a replica economy with its own source of high-level technology. Perhaps an economy can be said to reach a self-reproduction stage if it has the ability to generate or regenerate critical industries. (This, at least, seems to be the capacity attributed by urbanists of the Jacobs school to the largest and most vital cities.[d]) The concept is ephemeral, so perhaps the best way to approach it is via a constructed example. Thus we propose the following interpretation of a generalized developmental plan.

Definition: A plan for the bounded cellular space S consists of the following:

1. An initial configuration c giving the state indices of all nonquiescent cells in S at $t = 0$.
2. A class of transition and decision rules $g(c)$ which gives the ground rules of production, consumption, demographic behavior, etc. $g(c)$ can be considered the iron rules under which the system operates.
3. A class of rules $g'(c)$ which contains controls for policy intervention. $g'(c)$ could have been included in $g(c)$, except that it may be useful to separate out special instruments for outside guidance, e.g., a criterion for moving to a more complex production regime. There is no loss of generality here; c could have been prespecified to include a "secretariat" (computing capacity) or special decision systems. (See Chapter 7.)

---

[c]In most economic applications, cellular spaces will be bounded, so we need only concern ourselves with whether a particular configuration can reproduce itself some small finite number of times.

[d]Failures of self-reproduction are more obvious: the ghost town or the base town that dries up when the military moves out are classic examples.

112

4. A set of exogenous boundary rules. The boundary rules govern "trade" at the border or "migration" into the bounded field.

Let us now consider some contexts in which these conditions can operate. Imagine that a planner confronts the region shown in Figure 5-1a and there establishes the configuration c consisting of the population cluster P and the set I, an array of "intermediate" goods (regions in different laminations are drawn as distinct regions within a single cellular plane). In the transition to $t = 1$, the set I is transformed into $I_j \subset I$ and M, an array of "modern capital." This new configuration c_1 is interpreted as the first step in a production-accumulation steady state of growth. The process described corresponds to the design and construction of a "new town" complete with residences, social services, and industrial facilities. The town is then "started up" and thereafter allowed to run on its own. We could also liken the process to the initial stages of an economic development program—the installation of infrastructure and transitional indus- trial capacity. We can presume for the moment that the configuration c_1 is sustainable under $g(c)$ and $g'(c)$ for the foreseeable future.

Self-reproduction has a number of interpretations within this system. First,

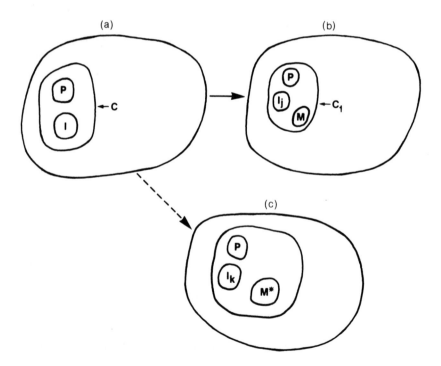

Figure 5-1. Planning Transformations

we could ask if c_1 can generate another configuration $c_1{}'$, a copy of c_1, which joins c_1 in steady-state production and accumulation. In effect, this is asking if a "new town" can spawn newer towns and thus general regional growth. The use of rules in $g'(c)$ would represent the prespecification of zoning regulations or the construction of communication and transportation networks to govern and guide the direction of growth under $g(c)$.

The second interpretation involves a type of "colonial" dependence. Suppose the new town was dependent upon trade with a military base (boundary condition) or the LDC was developing its industrial capacity to meet a particular export market; then the base moves or the market dries up. Does the configuration have the capacity to reorient itself to a new boundary condition? Or, in other terms, can the plan be wound back and the system returned to the initial state c? Figure 5-1c shows a new choice of development direction made from c; I is transformed into $I_k \subset I$ and M^*, the machinery base oriented to an alternate line of development.

In short, the self-reproduction issue turns on a number of elements: the richness of the mix of infrastructural elements installed in the initial configuration (or obtainable from it); the size of the configuration so as to allow the system to exceed critical thresholds for key resources or elements; and the inherent requirements of the existing technology. Clearly the critical size and complexity thresholds for trading and market cities in ancient Attica or Yucatan were of a different order of magnitude than those we might infer for contemporary technology.

Again, these matters are pure conjecture, but they do seem to define an intriguing area for developmental or historical study. It should be noted that although it seems impossible to define self-reproduction minimum levels of complexity on à-priori grounds, it is entirely reasonable to calculate empirical complexity measures that may give insights as to where and how such posited thresholds might operate. Of particular interest is the conjecture that advancing technology requires higher and higher self-reproduction thresholds.

The Garden of Eden Conjecture

Once we have gone this far down the byways of cellular-automata theory, it is worth examining an additional conjecture which emerges once one examines systems complicated enough to be capable of self-reproduction. This is the Garden of Eden characteristic proposed by Moore and demonstrated for a number of systems (including the game of Life).[e] Moore's Garden of Eden theorem proves the existence of configurations which are feasible under the rules and side conditions of a particular CA system, but which cannot be reached

[e]See *Lifeline* no. 3 for a demonstration. *Lifeline* is a mimeographed journal of game-of-Life studies published by R. Wainwright, Yorktown Heights, New York.

from any predecessor configuration. That is, a Garden of Eden configuration could exist only at $t = 0$. In the economic domain, this would be equivalent to a position which could exist under the rules of the system (defined as in the planning model earlier) but which could not be reached by any dynamic path. One way to formalize the notion is to propose that a general equilibrium, described as set of state descriptions (or as price and quantity vectors), might be a feasible solution of a system but might yet be an unattainable Garden of Eden position. Another example, which follows from the planning example, arises if we postulate an initial configuration and rules (say, Dallas and its chamber of commerce and zoning commission) and a solution point (say, Florence) and then face the problem that Florence may be a Garden of Eden never to be approximated with the existing Texas structures.

Of course, this and the preceding cases push the analogy to the limit. There is really no way of knowing at this time whether these notions can ever become operational within the social sciences.

6

A Parable of Development, Industrialization, and Increasing Complexity

As noted earlier, this chapter is a metaphorical excursion. It involves the use of primitive elements and naive forms to construct a model which passes through "stages" of development and exhibits characteristics which are thought to exemplify an advanced industrial system. In this sense, the chapter is a "parable" or "metaphor" of development. There is a formal and nontrivial aspect to the exercise, however; a number of propositions with serious theoretical content can be expressed in terms of the subject matter of the parable, and these propositions give insights into what can be proved or demonstrated within larger, more realistic SUR models. In a way, the analysis is an abstraction from the system outlined in Chapters 1 and 2 for a primitive economy. The starting point there was a cellular space labeled a "population plane" in which demographic and social relationships were worked out. The population plane was then combined with other laminar cellular spaces that represented the agricultural technology and production systems. In this chapter we will use even simpler elements to represent qualitatively similar behaviors.

We begin the parable with an exaggeratedly simple case in which we actually use game-of-Life rules (described in Appendix 1A and 1B) for the population plane and similar naive forms for other relationships. This convention is pedagogical and is followed in order to emphasize qualitative differences in structure rather than state or rule complexity. There is a heuristic lesson here, as well, in that abstract, stylized elements which are absurd on their own are shown to be quite capable of representing fairly elaborate and realistic relationships.[a]

The demographic plane is stipulated to be a composition of *stable life configurations* of the sort illustrated in Figure 6-1. Such units are labeled "tribes," and the individual cell elements are labeled "extended families." Under Life rules these configurations will remain in place, neither growing nor decreasing in size. The stable life configuration simulates a result obtained in the detailed LDC model of Chapter 2, but of course shows no structural detail. In the model of Chapter 2, groups of extended families form tribes under any of the following rule or state conditions: (1) A "wasteland" state exists for land, and the agricultural technology leads to build-up of fertilized land in the neighborhood of population accumulation and exhaustion of land at the

[a]This is also an attempt at a *tour de force*; the life rules form the simplest "mathematically interesting" CA model. It is obvious that life outcomes can be easily obtained by more elaborate and more realistic systems. To produce outcomes of economic significance with a system this austere demonstrates, we believe, the enormous representational power of the general methodology.

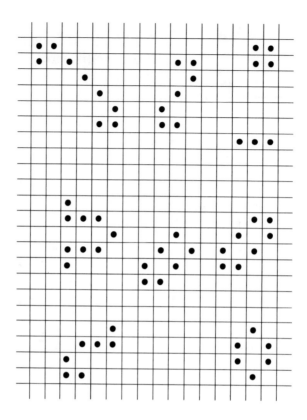

Figure 6-1. Some Stable Life Forms (Still Lifes).*

*A comprehensive file of life objects appears in the newsletter *Lifeline*, published by Robert Wainright, Yorktown Heights, New York.

periphery; (2) time costs are incurred in traveling to peripheral land; (3) there are strong social gains in organizing densely (e.g., bandits are modeled); (4) the configuration is forced by specifying wasteland boundaries as initial conditions.

The Life rules are retained in order to leave the model open to possible congestion effects from the building of technology and to loosely represent the agricultural technology within the demographic plane. (For example, there are density limits to the number of families within the plane under Life rules, and this suggests an upper limit to food production.) Enough though on this convention; we consider next rules for the accumulation of capital.

Capital in Production

First, a neighborhood is defined: Figure 6-2*a* is a "template" or pattern which is oriented to the cross-hatched cell, a representation of c_{kj} in capital space and c_{pj}

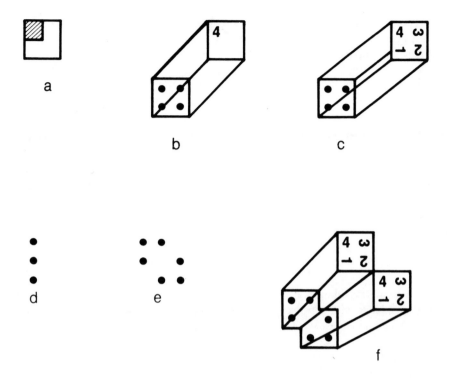

Figure 6-2. Simple Production of Capital

in population space. Where the template is moved through the population space, it describes the production neighborhood C_{pj} of c_{kj}. Now we introduce a rule to produce capital if the template "fits" the community, and an additional rule to govern the aging and accumulation of capital.

Rule 1. If three live cells are in C_{pj}, a unit of capital is created at c_{kj}; the unit of capital is given the state index "4," indicating its useful life. (The creation of a unit of capital is illustrated in Figure 6-2b; the cell with the index "4" is c_{kj}.)

Rule 2. Each live capital cell in year t shifted one unit to the right in $t + 1$; its orientation is turned $-90°$ and its index reduced. (Figure 6-2c shows the position after 4 "years," at which point a "steady state" is reached—a sustainable capital stock of 4 units is obtained from the "economic surplus" of the tribe.[b])

[b]This is a stylized version of the aging functions for Chapter 2. The displacements and rotations are merely tricks to keep capital from piling up on itself.

The rules are not restricted to the particular block tribal configuration illustrated in Figure 6-2*a* to *c*. Figure 6-2*e* shows a tribe (an oscillating cluster) that is "ineffective" in production, that is, the given template cannot produce a "fit" in the population plane. The tribe illustrated in Figure 6-2*e* can produce an interesting result. If we change the rules slightly and allow the capital neighborhood to be offset from the population neighborhood, we can reach the position illustrated in Figure 6-2*f*. This tribe is more "efficient" than the original block formation (where efficiency is measured as output of capital per population element). Formalizing this observation, we have Theorem 6-1. Calling this a "theorem" is admittedly puffery, but a purpose of this chapter is to codify intuitive notions of structure. Clearly no proof beyond the demonstration just presented is needed for this and the following theorem.

THEOREM 6-1. Certain production regimes are most efficient for particular arrangements of population, and, conversely, particular population arrangements will call for the design of appropriate production technology.[c]

Rules and neighborhood relationships of the sort illustrated can be put into correspondence with a particular technique of handcraft production. According to the technique in use, we have Theorem 6-2.

THEOREM 6-2. Communities of particular sizes and spatial orientation will have relative advantages in terms of (1) the speed in which they reach K*, the maximal-sustainable capital stock (a steady-state value, in which the total capital stock and its age structure remain stable over time), and (2) the efficiency of economic organization (productivity is measured as K* per capita).

This simple production model applies quite obviously to handcraft technology and a tribal or communal stage of development. The next stage in the parable is a move to a more advanced economy that incorporates production functions of standard types.

Production Sequences

Hierarchic production sequences can be represented in the system with a simple alteration of the rules. "Machines" are produced by a handcraft technique similar to those above (the rules for making machines can be on the stringent

---

[c]The analysis appears to have useful applications within ethnography and economic anthropology in that it points to correspondences between characteristics of primitive technology and social forms that are efficient with respect to such technology. The problem of "structure" is a focus of controversy within anthropology, and this is hardly the place to enter the debate in a serious way. It is simply noted that the formulations here are consistent with the view of economic structure proposed by Levi-Strauss (p. 274).

side for emphasis). Then a new set of rules is devised for production that employs both labor and machines. In effect, the rules set up a production function for labor and capital that satisfies predetermined joint-neighborhood conditions.

Let us, for example, label the capital plane as "knives" and assume that knives both are valued for their own sake and can be used as capital in carving out other items. Suppose now that an emissary of a trading company arrives on the scene and declares a willingness to trade knives for masks (which will be sold in advanced countries as examples of primitive art). Masks are carved by people working with knives, according to the rules illustrated in Figure 6-3. Figure 6-3a is a template which operates in the population plane; Figure 6-3b operates in the capital plane. These templates define production neighborhoods C_{pi} and C_{ki} which are oriented to c_{mi}, a reference cell in the mask plane (a higher lamination). Rules for producing masks are as follows:

Rule M_1: At least 4 live cells must exist in C_{pi}.

Rule M_2: At least 3 units of capital must be present in C_{kj}.

Rule M_3 : If M_1 and M_2, then M, the number of masks which can be produced in c_{mi}, is a function of the number of persons (N), in C_{pi}, and knives (K) in C_{ki}—(sample rules might be $\log M = a_1 \log N + a_2 \log K$, etc.).

The trader acquaints the tribe with these production facts and also P^*, a trading ratio of knives for masks. If $P^*M > K^*$ (where, again, K^* is steady-state

a   b   c

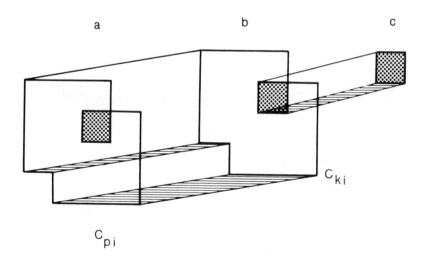

Figure 6-3. Capital in Production

knife production under hand-labor conditions), the tribe may be convinced to produce for trade using the roundabout technique. Although the price ratio is given from outside the system, in effect one models an economic decision to produce or not to produce. (Again, one could just as well include a market that determines P^* within a larger SUR model.) It is clear that one can fix the value of P^* so that production will be economic for all villages at or above the minimum stable size or just for those villages which are large enough to gain some production advantages. A simple numerical example (Figure 6-4) may help to demonstrate this: in Figure 6-4a we see a production template (with a "hole") applied to the standard "block" village. Total feasible production is figured for an assumed Cobb-Douglas function $M = N^{1/2} \cdot K^{1/2}$. In this case, production is calculated to be 4 units (or 1 unit per capita). Feasible mask production for the larger village (of Figure 6-2e is 6.926 units, or 1.154 units per capita. Using conventional calculations, we find that price ratios which will generate a switch to the roundabout technique are $P^* > 1$ for the block village and $P^* > 0.87$ for the larger village, which is capable of greater production efficiency under the existing regime.

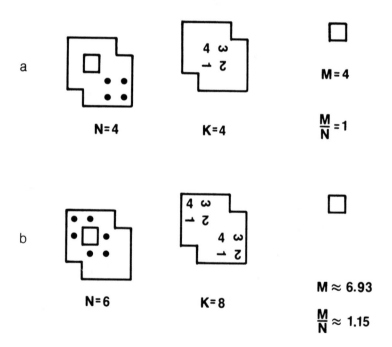

Figure 6-4. Production under a Cobb-Douglas Regime.

Technical Change and External Effects

Although this example is contrived, naive, and heavily reliant on an integer construct, it should be clear that we are simply simulating types of threshold constructs which are quite reasonable in terms of models presented earlier. For example, we might specify demographic labor-force subclassifications within the larger population groupings and rely on the rules and neighborhood relationships to determine whether production was feasible. However, once we have gone this far toward capital-using development in our parable, we should recognize other production potentialities of a more fundamental nature. These are loosely described as (1) technological change associated with increased roundaboutness, (2) technological change associated with increased communication or with the extension of production neighborhoods, (3) congestion or pollution diseconomies associated with advanced modes of production, and (4) investment and infrastructure requirements of advanced development. Discussion of these matters follows—but with less formality than the parallel exposition of Chapter 4.

Technological Change through
Increased Roundaboutness

The previous section gave a simple example of this type of technological change; we will now consider the general case. Suppose that instead of "masks," knife capital were used to produce "machine" capital. Then the third lamination could be labeled the "machinery plane," and rules for the accumulation of machinery could be specified. A production function ranging over the joint machinery and population neighborhoods is specified next; the accumulation rule and production function would be similar in nature to those described in the previous section; and final product would be produced in a still higher lamination. The interesting cases are where the roundabout technique is more productive than its predecessor, so that accumulation to deepen capital is potentially an economic proposition.

The necessary calculations are straightforward: first we should seek a quantifiable notion of "productivity" and then consider decision rules. We designate Q_s as maximum production of final product at the level of the sth lamination. This production level obtains where the maximum sustainable capital at this level is associated with the locally available labor force (assumed equal to N units). Technique s is more productive than technique r if $Q_s/N > Q_r/N$, where roundaboutness is indicated by $s > r$. Price ratios can determine whether a switch to the more roundabout technique is economic (as in the previous section) and whether the implied investment decision should be made. This, of course, takes us to the point at which the adjective "neo-Austrian" becomes meaningful, and we can drop the expositional artifice of bringing in our prices from abroad. We have left the economic magnitudes of the system unspecified; and we, in effect, have complete freedom to specify distributional and pricing mechanisms. Note that the model gives us a complete count and labeling of machines and outputs (but where the final output is undesignated). It is reasonable, in developing the representation of an LDC village economy that is peripheral in relation to the industrial core of the economy, to stick with the open-economy associations. However, we can treat the model system as self-contained; in this instance we have a designated final product (and agricultural product) but freedom to select both a set of values (or prices) and a pattern of income distribution. We even have the freedom to designate and label the actors in the scheme. It is not our purpose to enter capital and distributional controversies at this point, and so the reader is given license to label according to taste. It is obvious, though, that these freedoms are sufficient to pick equilibrium configurations of the system. Theorem 6-3 codifies these observations.

THEOREM 6-3 (a). A system based on parametric automata specifying only agricultural production and the sequence of production can be put into correspondence with a neo-Austrian production sequence. This follows from the definition of a neo-Austrian sequence as the relationship of dated outputs to dated inputs of machines (quasi-machines) which are recursively associated with an input of pure labor at some initial period.

(b) The automata version of the model allows complete freedom for selection of distributional and value bases.

(c) The extension of roundaboutness is equivalent to a laminar technical change as defined in Chapter 4.

(d) At any point of time and for any set of values (or prices), one can compute the choice of sequence that will be followed by the economy.

Technological Change through Extension of Production Neighborhoods

Continuing with the parable, let us now consider the possibility of building a "factory" between two villages and there assembling the available labor and capital for production at a predefined level of roundaboutness. Factory production is represented in the model by a larger production neighborhood (the template illustrated in Figure 6-5 should be compared with that in Figure 6-2), and naturally we are concerned with the case in which factor productivity is higher with the technique that extends over wider neighborhoods. Again a

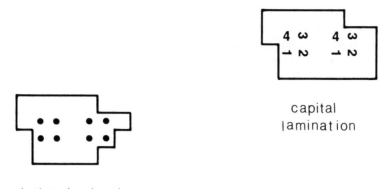

capital
lamination

population lamination

Figure 6-5. An Extended Production Neighborhood

numerical example may be helpful. We deal with a Cobb-Douglas function as before, but now we assume the form $M = aN^{\frac{1}{2}}K^{\frac{1}{2}}$, where $a > 1$ for the wider production neighborhood. Additional investment might be required to introduce this technique, and the technique might be economic only for particular arrangements and densities of population.

This description can be codified:

THEOREM 6-4. Scale phenomena can be represented as an extension of neighborhood with an altered production rule. The effect will almost surely be nonparametric (Chapter 4), but the decision to adopt or not to adopt an altered technology and rule structure is subject to representation and programming. (The effects of the new technology, whether anticipated or not, are also representable.) Thus it is possible to model and represent most of the salient aspects of a full sequence of development and structural change.

Congestion and Pollution Diseconomies

The parable presents technical change as a movement to a deeper, more roundabout technique or an extension of a technique to a wider production neighborhood. These are familiar concepts, and there are obvious evocations of externalities and scale phenomena in the model representation. It is natural, then, to ask how the model can be used to represent the other side of technological progress: usurpation of living space and corruptive externalities. We stipulate now that a cell in the population space can assume, along with the "live" and "quiescent" states, a third state which we will label "clogged." Each quiescent cell c_{pi} has a neighborhood C_{pi}^{E} which extends through all higher machine laminations. If the concentration of active cells in $C_{pi}^{\dot{E}}$ exceeds a predetermined limit, c_{pi} becomes clogged. The rule which establishes population limits applies to clogged cells, but clogged cells have no productive power. In effect, production facilities—machines, factories, communication and transportation networks—take up living space and ultimately displace life. That is, for a suitable choice of boundary conditions and technology rules, the model can precisely mimic Los Angeles or Belgium. It is interesting to note that at one moment of time the economy can be active and life full of material blessings; but with the next extension and ramification of technique, clogging becomes critical and physical existence impossible. A few time steps later, all that would be left is the machine superstructure with insufficient population to make it operative. Given present concern with environmental problems, it is a fair expectation that the model will be widely adopted for the representation of polluting processes. In this context, we should stress the ease with which cellular models can portray threshold effects (the reader should recall Figure 1-1h). It is hard to think of any conventional treatment of growth that can produce this type of phenomenon.[d]

Again, codifying the discussion, we have Theorem 6-5.

THEOREM 6-5. Any sequence of nonparametric change will generate a history of computable complexity parameters. Following an argument presented in Chapter 4, some of these parameters will be associated with ecological and environmental effects. A development sequence, however, can be associated with jumps in the values of derived environmental and congestion variables; these jumps may imply irreversible movements past critical thresholds. (Such jumps may or may not be predictable using standard projection and extrapolation techniques.)

Investment Requirements Associated
with Technological Advance

The parable of historical development has the tribal village advancing to a higher level of factor productivity by moving to a more roundabout, capital-based technology. Thus far we have skirted the basic problem of intermediate capital goods: that is, if workers use knives to make masks or machines, who makes the knives? One way to treat this matter is to allow regeneration of intermediate

---

[d]It is not difficult to derive the clogging implications of many real-world technological extensions. Take the SST for an example. This technique links two production neighborhoods (New York-London or Los Angeles-Sydney), but in order to realize the potentialities of the technique, one would have to link a remote airport to city centers with a high-speed transportation link on the surface. The required displacement of already congested living space is readily calculated (without even taking into account upper-atmosphere pollution, noise, and opportunity uses of subsidies).

goods in the rules for more roundabout production. An alternate approach with interesting developmental implications sets up the rules so that intermediate capital must, in effect, come from abroad in the early stages of industrialization; in this case the model becomes the framework for a structural model of international factor movements. This approach appears as a potentially fruitful subject for further applied study, no specific theorems are introduced at this time.

One can take a similar view on technological advances associated with extensions of production neighborhoods. Suppose that the broadening of neighborhoods to include two population clusters requires that a "road" be built between them. The road can be explicitly modeled and analyzed in terms of its clogging implications; it can also be analyzed in terms of its implied investment requirements. Again, we can program the rules so that these requirements must be met from abroad, in which case we come very close to expressing a colonial or branch-dependency relationship. A separate "colonial investment" account can be kept, recording infrastructure and intermediate-capital placements. These accounts would be calculated in a separate model for the colonial interest—distinct from the cellular scheme. Price ratios in the colonial power—an economy already at an advanced stage of roundaboutness and infrastructure develop-ment—can be such that investment from outside is economic while investment in intermediate goods by the dependent country is not. This version of the "absorptive capacity" limitation can be demonstrated with some rigor and is certainly a promising area for simulation.

Conclusions

The sermon on the lessons to be drawn from the parable will be brief. The examples and theorems presented in this chapter were designed to be suggestive and provocative. A single-model type was used as the setting for a long historical or developmental sequence which involved substantial qualitative change and structural adaptation. Simple forms were used, but it was clear that these forms could be elaborated to any desired level of detail while still preserving basic qualitative structure.

There are still many substantive issues to consider. It is not yet clear what levels of complexity are required, in practice, to initiate a development sequence, nor is it clear how or whether the self-reproduction characteristic (Chapter 5) is an aspect of system development. The parable raises issues and potentialities, but at the very least we have a system that integrates considerable and varied bodies of theory and analysis inside and outside economics.

7

An Excursion into Social-choice Theory

Thus far we have treated automata theory as a means of description and as a basis for structural analysis. In this chapter we will step off in quite a different direction and consider applications of automata theory in pure welfare economics. Let it be clear at the outset that except for general mathematical method there is only the thinnest thread of connection between earlier materials and those we will consider now. The purpose of this chapter is to illustrate a use of cellular-automata methodology within a quite different conceptual setting, in the hope that this application will demonstrate more of the range and power of the technique. There is no attempt here to develop comprehensive welfare economics, nor will we even consider many of the lines into choice theory that are suggested by various versions of the CA model.[a]

The specific line we will consider derives from the use of CA formulations in determining the computability of functions. The matter is at the foundation level in mathematical logic and extends from the work of Gödel and Turing. (See the Appendix to the Introduction for a detailed description of the Turing machine concept.) In the computerscience literature, the issue appears as the "computability" or "halting" problem. We begin with the argument that the standard social-choice criteria and decision procedures are, by their very nature, computable routines. But we ask whether a welfare analysis that predicts the outcome of such computable processes is itself computable and therefore determinate.

The Problem

This chapter takes an unusual tack in its consideration of some basic existence problems in welfare economics. A classic approach in pure welfare theory involves proposing a decision rule, ranking criterion or evaluation procedure, and then checking the conformity of that rule with general tests of logical consistency, equity, or reasonableness. Thus we have the following: (1) The

[a]The work of Piccoli, cited earlier, is an imaginative application in choice theory of cellular automata used to represent the language of social decisions. There is also a considerable body of work in "pattern recognition" which is suggestive as to the logic of communication within decentralized systems, while other signaling applications are suggested by work on the organization of neural receptors using CA elements. On signaling problems, generally, see Albin (1971) and Hurwicz. References to work on neural systems appear in Minsky's text.

127

127

Arrow impossibility theorem which demonstrates that no procedure for arraying social settlements can be guaranteed to pass a minimally restrictive test of consistency with the ordering of individual preference; (2) a considerable literature following Hicks, Kaldor, and Scitovsky which shows that "index number" and/or "compensation" tests of welfare improvements may not be definitive; and (3) a literature on the "second best" which demonstrates the failure possibilities of various bureaucratic decision criteria for public activities. (These topics have been surveyed repeatedly, as, for example, in Sen's distinguished text.)

It is, of course, well known that the social-decision apparatus need not fail. There are many instances in which an election or other procedure covered by the Arrow theorem will perform quite adequately. Similarly, there can be outcomes which register as unambiguous gains under the index-number or compensation tests. Finally, there can be cases where we are quite satisfied with the outcomes of standard decision criteria. One hopes for such a clean decision environment; nevertheless, in the real world choices have to be made, even where welfare ambiguities are known to be present.

It is part of the traditional approach to attempt to discover what is or might be lost in the course of actual events and practical politics. For example, one might judge that a particular outcome is only "satisfactory" if the evaluater adopts a degraded set of decision criteria or accepts a weaker set of conditions on decision rules. [See, for example, Campbell (1973) for discussion centering on restrictions on "irrelevant alternatives."] It might also turn out that a decision was reached only because of the exclusion of particular constituencies or because a particular set of choices was pared out of a broader choice set, so that the actual decision was made on a restricted domain.[b] In such cases the decision is, in effect, an accomplished fact. The issue is to discover the extent to which one must compromise one's standards in order to judge the outcome as acceptable. The problem could be put a bit less pessimistically as well. Suppose, one places extremely rigid requirements on a decision process, e.g., the specific outcome should satisfy Arrow, should pass a rigid compensation test (on the prior and postdistributions of welfare), and should pass a few bureaucratic guidelines as well. Could we not ask if we can obtain a practical outcome that meets some of but not necessarily all the restrictions?

In principle, a welfare evaluation (in terms of the extent to which standards are degraded) could be calculated for any outcome, and, in principle, one should also be able to calculate what outcomes might follow a specific relaxation of restrictions on decision procedures.[c] The question we will consider, however,

[b]Note that the Arrow theorem will still apply for these restricted choices. We are saying that no inconsistency arises in the specific *post*restriction choice situation.

[c]Note we are limiting ourselves to finite decision domains, i.e., the Arrow enumeration of states and choice-makers. The question of social choice is of practical interest only if the possibility of rational calculation is present.

concerns both of these aspects simultaneously. Could a welfare economist be given (1) an initial position for a political-economic system, (2) a statement of the decision rules employed in the system, and (3) a stipulation of standards including ways in which they might be relaxed under pressure, and on the basis of this information determine the welfare standards which apply to the post-decision-process position? This would seem to be an interesting line for welfare analysis for the following reasons:

1. It leads directly into consideration of the steps and actions taken in the decision process.
2. It allows simultaneous consideration of decision rules along with other standards and criteria.[d]
3. It emphasizes the characteristics of a position actually reached.
4. It permits direct analysis of the dynamic adjustments of a political system, most notably a system in crisis.
5. It formalizes the position of the welfare economist in an evaluative role outside of the system itself.

We have proposed what appears to be a reasonable description of a field for social decisions and of the functional role of a welfare economist in evaluating decisions made within the field. The question now is that of discovering the extent to which that function can be accomplished. As might be expected, the answer turns out to be a negative one—that there is no guarantee that welfare assessments can be made. The impossibility proof does not depend in any way on the Arrow logic and result, but derives simply from an enumeration of what is possible and what is not possible to compute. The subject is one for general automata since we will be concerned with computable procedures in a field which is itself described as a composition of finite automata (e.g., a generalized activity and preference model). We begin by describing the field and then turn to the problem of describing decision processes over the field. Formal proofs are

---

[d]As Arrow and Campbell have demonstrated, the decision rule can easily be generalized to cover such elements as compensatory side payments. A test such as that suggested by Scitovsky (i.e., that side payments do not reverse a choice already made) involves additional restrictions. For example, take the familiar case (amplified by Campbell) of a bridge intensely desired by a minority, but moderately disliked by a majority. If the status quo is state x and the economy with the bridge is state y (making up with other conditions to set S), it may well be that $x P y$. If, however, we permit side payments, a state (or class of states) Z is introduced, where Z involves a bribe of certain members of the majority. Under these conditions, the bridge may go through, but it is clear that the impossibility theorem has not been bypassed since the Arrow dilemma could hold in the state set S' that is expanded by the elements Z. But now let us say that we run into no Arrow problems for S' but that the stricter Scitovsky requirements bite for a particular set of side payments that give the state Z'. (That is, in Z' the population would want to buy back X.) We ask if the actual decision process leaves a result that would satisfy both Scitovsky and Arrow or whether one might end up sacrificing Scitovsky, leaving us with Arrow alone or even a weaker form of Arrow.

given in Appendix 7A, but the line of proof is identical to that given earlier (Appendix to the Introduction) for Turing machine automata and the halting problem.

The Formal Analysis

State Descriptions

Following Arrow's usage, we define a *state of the economy* as a complete description covering all activities, all processes, all income receipts, present and future. A less-than-complete description $\hat{s}$ is permissible, and the state set S can contain s'', a technically infeasible case (e.g., a utopia) as well as feasible states s'_j. The only condition on S is that it be finite. We may wish to distinguish s_0 which is the status quo or s^* which is another feasible state taken for purposes of reference. (For example, s^* might be a state which obtained in the remembered past or a state which is prominent as an alternative.)

Opinions and Individual Preferences

Each individual i possesses a preference function F_i. However, no restrictions are placed on the form of F. We say that

$$F_{i0} \rightarrow s_{j0}{}^i \tag{7.1}$$

meaning that in the zeroth (status quo) period, individual i assigns an index number to the state j. More generally, we can have

$$F_{ik} \rightarrow s_{jk}{}^i \tag{7.2}$$

which is the assignment of index numbers which would occur if the choice were to be made in state k. (This is a relevant consideration were we to take a Kaldor view on welfare comparisons.) O is the set of all opinions $s_{jk}{}^i$. Since i, j, and k are finite, O will contain a finite number of elements. In practical politics, O will be imperfectly known and may consist of a small collection of data on poll results, previous election returns, letters to members of Congress, position papers, and the like. Alternatively, we may say that O consists of a complete ordering over individuals and states and vantage points. Either interpretation is permissible in what follows.

Social Welfare Operations and
Politics

$W(O)$ is a social welfare operation or "political process." In effect, $W(O)$ assigns an index w_j to a state j in S, according to information in O:

$$W(O) \rightarrow w_j \quad \text{for some } j \tag{7.3}$$

and suggests an ordering R over some such states

$$R_{jk} = w_j \cdot R \cdot w_k \quad \text{for some } j, k \tag{7.4}$$

Equation (7.4) could subsume variously a social welfare function in the form of a field of social indifference curves, a full rank ordering of the elements in S, or a partial ordering covering, say, a small set of pairwise comparisons of elements in S.

Welfare Outcomes

An outcome or ranking $R_{jk} = w_j R w_k$ is *acceptable* if it satisfies some prespecified welfare criterion L^x, where L^x may take any of these forms:

$$L^x = \text{any of} \quad \begin{aligned} L^O &= L^O\,(R_{jk}, O) \\ L^S &= L^S\,(R_{jk}, S) \\ L^l &= L^l\,(R_{jk}, O_l) \\ L^I &= L^I\,(R_{jk}, I) \\ L^Y &= L^Y\,(R_{jk}, Y) \end{aligned} \tag{7.5}$$

For example, L^O might be the restriction that the ranking R_{jk} satisfy the Arrow axioms, which are, in effect, a condition depending upon O. A quite unrestricted version of L^O is the condition that R_{jk} satisfy *one* person's ranking; this would permit the dictatorship outcome.

A version of L^S would be the condition that if s_j dominates s_k according to some prespecified criterion, $s_k \rightarrow s_j$ is unacceptable. This is a completely general Pareto rule.

L^l could be the restriction that a ranking R_{jk} should be preserved whether the vantage point was the status quo or some other state indexed by l. L^I consists of an ideological restriction, based, say, on the red book. L^Y is some unspecified restriction, reasonable or not (note that L^Y might include restrictions requiring that the rankings under R be transitive, or that Rawlsian justice should obtain).

We now have L as the set of all conditions L^X, and we set up the problem in this way: A specific condition or set of conditions, L^*, is selected from L, and we ask if the political process will produce a ranking consistent with L^*. If L^* is particularly unrestrictive, the political process will produce a consistent ranking almost immediately (as would be the case were the dictatorship outcome permitted under L^* and one began with a dictatorship). The more interesting cases, of course, are ones in which the conditions in L^* are rich and demanding; in such cases one cannot have advance confidence that an outcome, R_{jk}, will be acceptable.

A General Recursive Political Process

We define a political *program* as an attempt to realize consistency between a social ordering R_{jk} (which need not be complete over all jk) and a prespecified condition L^*. The program consists of a series of steps of the following types.

v_0 = search over S

v_1 = eliminating from consideration the opinions o_i of certain individuals. This involves recalculating R on information in O' a subset of O.

v_2 = eliminating particular states from consideration and thus in effect attempting to obtain consistency over a reduced domain of alternatives, e.g., for R'_{jk} such that $s_j, s_k \in S' \subset S$

v_3 = alteration of the ranking function $W(O)$ by selecting an alternative version from the (finite) set of functions

v_4 = picking a less restrictive criterion L^*

A specific program P then consists of an enumeration of steps to be followed in attempting to obtain consistency. We note the following characteristics of a program:

1. The steps associated with any of the categories $V = (v_0, v_1, v_2, v_3, v_4)$ are finite in number and consist of a permutation over the relevant elements: individuals and sets of individuals (for v_1); states and sets of states (for v_0 and v_2); and selections from a finite list of functions (for v_3 and v_4).
2. A specific program describes a composition of permutations over finite elements and is thus an element of a well-defined finite group.

This description of a political program, although abstract and general, translates into actual politics. Consider the problem of a parliamentary democracy in crisis. The search for a constituency base can proceed from attempts to form various coalitions. Such attempts are, in classic political terms, attempts to find viable exclusions over individuals. The attempt to resolve the crisis may also involve admitting or excluding certain states from political discourse (e.g., all major parties stop talking about states that involve a high rate of economic growth and limit discourse to states which simply maintain the system). The attempts may also bring in constitutional changes or *de facto* changes in the basic understandings concerning political roles. Finally, the standards of permissible operations held both by inside observers (permitting moves toward extraordinary powers or dictatorship) and by outside observers (shifting from an "efficiency" criterion of evaluation to a "stability" criterion) may change. One can develop further associations between the abstract system and actual procedures, but there is every reason to argue that the abstract description allows a close-to-complete representation of political behaviors.[e]

Political Effectiveness

We state that a program P is *effective* if, after some number of steps in its prearranged sequence, an acceptable correspondence between R and L is reached. This definition applies variously to a dictatorship that sets its program after one consultation with the dictator, a democracy that forms a consensus after several rounds of debate, logrolling, wheeling and dealing, and a parliamentary system that downgrades its objectives and standards and ends up with a government under emergency powers after a sequence of attempts to form more palatable regimes.

At last we are nearly at the problem: we first define a pundit. *A pundit is a sage who can predict whether a program will be effective.* Specifically, the pundit will predict how many steps N it will take to complete P_p, a particular selection from the class P^{**}.

Now, what is the meaning of this construction? If a pundit can take a particular program and see that it will take N_1 steps to complete, then the pundit will, in effect, have determined the set of conditions over which a political process can lead to an acceptable result. This includes a selection of criteria in L, a selection of an effective constituency in O, and a restriction of

---

[e]We should also consider certain other operations such as (1) augmenting the set of states by permitting transfer or tax changes that form new states from the initial set S, or (2) operating on F (through propaganda?). These options increase the domain of political activity beyond all bounds and therefore turn the operation P into an infinite group. Since our primary result consists of an inherent limitation to welfare evaluations for a finite group, opening things up in this way can only strengthen the result.

the field in S. This appears, then, to be as general a description of a welfare economist as one might wish to have, and we progress inevitably to an existence theorem.

THEOREM: There is no pundit.

A number of readers may have anticipated the theorem. We have described a political process as a program which could, in principle, be computed. The question of the existence of a pundit thus corresponds to a question of computability—specifically, the halting problem—the question of whether a computer can be programmed to predict that a particular class of a problem can or cannot be solved by a subject program. The theorem is shown in many forms (see, for example, Minsky in Chapter 8) and is in fact a development of Gödel's methods, using Turing's abstraction of a computing machine. The proof stated in Appendix 7A is a paraphrase of a proof by Thatcher in Burks (1970).

An example will be helpful at this point. Suppose we have a political system with a finite number of individuals and a finite number of states. We apply, as a standard of acceptability, consistency with the Arrow axioms (A) *and* consistency with the Kaldor-Scitovsky criterion (K). That is, the program must satisfy ordering consistency under (A) and meet a further requirement that the ordering must also stand up when viewed from the postchange position.

The search for an acceptable proposal could have any of the following outcomes.

P_1 (very strong) = finding a proposal that satisfies $(A + K)$ for the image of the full electorate O and choice set S.

P_2 (not so strong) = finding a proposal that satisfies $(A + K)$ but for a reduced electorate $O' \subset O$ and/or reduced choice space $S' \subset S$.

P_3 (weak) = finding a proposal that satisfies A or K for the full electorate O and full choice set S.

P_4 (very weak) = finding a proposal that satisfies A *or* K but for a reduced electorate $O' \subset O$ and/or reduced choice space $S' \subset S$.

P_5 (degraded) = finding a proposal that satisfies a degraded criterion: e.g., dictatorship (D)

The pundit theorem states the impossibility of predicting in general which of P_1 to P_5 will obtain. The theorem does allow some limited punditing. For example, if one knows that there exists an outcome at the P_v level which is acceptable and can be reached by a program (e.g., a three-person electorate that produces acceptable rankings and that selections and eliminations will ultimately define this set), then one can predict that there will be no further degradation to P_5, but one cannot predict which P_4 will obtain or whether some superior program P_1 to P_3 will hold.

Comments and Conclusions

There is some small temptation to stop here and leave the problem of interpretation and application to the reader. A few points, however, should clarify the result.

1. The pundit theorem does not invalidate any specific finding of consistency or nonconsistency between policy outcomes and a criterion system. It is obvious that policy outcomes in an absolute monarchy are constrained only by technology, so no punditry is needed for such a case.
2. The pundit theorem can be considered as an extension of Arrow's famous result (as currently amended). An impossibility theorem is extended over a more general class of axioms; and, for the Arrow case itself, the theorem shows that there is no guarantee that a sequence of adjustments from an initial position inconsistent with the axioms will terminate in a satisfactory outcome.
3. Potentially, the most important contribution of the construction is the description of stepwise political adjustments and policy accommodations. This procedure satisfies intuition as to the nature of adjustments in the face of a crisis of serious political discrepancies—the case which should be the referent for discussions in the spirit of Arrow.
4. The stepwise construction of political and policy accommodations can be extended to other welfare problems. A successor paper will consider the specific problem of calculating the potential welfare gains from an iterative sequence of adjustments.
5. Analytical methodology based on a computability criterion seems appropriate to a broad class of welfare problems. Note that the welfare "operations" treated in this paper subsume Bergson-type social welfare functions, and both complete and incomplete rankings for program evaluations. There is also a feeling that if "rational choice" is to be distinguished from inspirational or metaphysical decision-making, computability must be the distinguishing characteristic.[f]

[f]M.L. Piccoli (1973) explains how an abstract automaton has the capacity to calculate whether a specific program satisfies the Arrow axioms. Her demonstration constitutes a full and rigorous proof of the computability of the types of calculation assumed here.

Appendix 7A:
Proof of the Pundit
Theorem

We begin by "numbering" programs in the political or policy domains according to the following scheme. The operation of eliminating or selecting an individual from O is labeled θ; that of eliminating or selecting a state from S, Σ; that of eliminating or selecting a function from W, Φ; and that of eliminating or selecting a criterion from L, λ. A program is thus an ordering, for example, $(\theta, \theta, \Sigma, \theta, \theta, \phi, \theta)$, of operations each of which could be coded into a computer routine.[a] We number lexographically beginning with all one-step programs, passing to two-step programs, three-step programs, etc. In this way each program is assigned a natural (Gödel) number; and, of course, we can quickly identify a program P_n with n steps from its placement on the long list.

Now we define the function h

$$h(n, m) = \begin{cases} 0 & \text{if } P_n \text{ with input } m \text{ stops} \\ 1 & \text{if } P_n \text{ with input } m \text{ does not stop} \end{cases} \tag{7A.1}$$

"Stopping" is understood to mean computing a consistency between L and R, where m is a specific numerical input drawn from O. The question of the existence of a pundit, then, depends on the computability of h. h computable implies that a pundit could predict that *some* program at the P_N level would generate an acceptable political outcome. This is, of course, an *essential* prerequisite to selection of the specific program and its implied restrictions. We are not really stepping too far afield in taking this line of proof. Choice by means other than magic or charisma involves calculation, and this must mean that a choice procedure is computable, at least in principle.

Computability implies specifically that the function h can be computed by a computer program (algorithm, language, and machine) which we label H. Thus,

$$n, m \xrightarrow{H} \begin{cases} 0 & \text{if } P_n \text{ stops with } m \\ 1 & \text{if } P_n \text{ does not stop} \end{cases} \tag{7A.2}$$

To test computability, we first describe an auxiliary function L:

$$\left. \begin{matrix} 0 \\ 1 \end{matrix} \right\} \xrightarrow{L} \begin{cases} \text{Does not stop} \\ \\ \text{Stops} \end{cases}$$

---

[a]We could, if we wished, subscript the operations to make them specific as to the elimination or selection intended.

i.e., if a given tape record is 0, the program loops to some address; if the record reads otherwise (e.g., contains 1), L causes the program to halt.

A second auxiliary function is I, which controls machine iterations through an adding routine. Thus

$$m, n \quad \underset{I}{\rightarrow} \quad m, n + m$$

or

$$n, 0 \quad \underset{I}{\rightarrow} \quad n, n \quad \underset{I}{\rightarrow} \quad n, 2n \quad \underset{I}{\rightarrow} \quad n, 3n$$

Now we consider the program H' which operates on the input m and is the composition of programs I, H, L. Thus,

$$m, 0 \quad \underset{I}{\rightarrow} \quad m, m \quad \underset{H}{\rightarrow} \quad \left\{ \begin{array}{ll} 0 & \text{if } P_m \text{ stops on } m \\ 1 & \text{if } P_m \text{ does not stop} \end{array} \right\} \quad \underset{L}{\rightarrow} \quad \left\{ \begin{array}{l} \text{no stop} \\ \text{stop} \end{array} \right. \quad (7A.3)$$

H' must have a number (assigned as in the case of P_n); choose the number m_0 so that H' stops with m_0. Then from Equation (7A.3) it follows that P_{m0} does *not* stop with input m_0. However, P_{m0} is H'—compare Equation (7A.2). Thus the construction is contradictory, particularly if we state it in the form "H' does not stops $\Rightarrow H'$ stops." We have thus demonstrated that the computing problem which must be solved by the pundit is in fact *unsolvable*. Lest it be felt that we have stacked the cards against the pundit, it should be stressed that the line of proof chosen here is among the most general constructions in the literature on the computability of functions and the solvability of systems. The proof in all important respects corresponds to the general proof of the halting problem given in the Appendix to the Introduction.

8 Conclusions

The preceding chapters establish equivalences between a large class of economic models and a general class of automata forms, including particularly the cellular-automaton model. The economic models include the various activity-analysis model types which are, by definition, automata, a large class of simulating models, general-equilibrium forms which include a social-decision mechanism. Furthermore, the automaton seems to be a meaningful metaphor for an economic unit—albeit, one without culture or personality—so that there is little strain on the intuition in putting forward the equivalency. Now, what can we make of these equivalencies or identifications?

(1) In some instances the equivalence has no practical impact on economic analysis, although it may be of mathematical interest. For example, describing a problem that is effectively solved by linear programming as a cellular-automaton problem would not significantly change solution procedures or value interpretations. Taking another viewpoint, nothing is learned here that would invalidate established results.

(2) In other instances, describing a problem in an automaton framework suggests theoretical formulations that would not otherwise be apparent. In this category are alternative solution concepts, theorems on self-reproduction and Garden-of-Eden uniqueness. It is not yet known whether these conditions apply to existing models, but they would seem to be apposite for models which might be constructed and, by extension, apposite for the economy itself.

(3) On the positive side, there are immediate and practical lines for empirical analysis that emerge from taking the metaphor seriously. Complexity measurement fits in this category. Quantitative assessment of the complexity of a system or subsystem was not previously perceived to be a problem within the domain of economic analysis. The fact that complexity analysis is a valid procedure within a parallel and equivalent methodology forces attention on the issue. Whether the issue merits attention and whether meaningful findings on system complexity can be obtained by application of the technique are matters which only experience will resolve.

(4) Going further, the equivalences are most encouraging for projects aiming at detailed representation of microunits and heuristic examination of their behaviors. The potentialities for representing physical capital, externalities, threshold effects, and structural changes are most favorable for this line.

(5) The equivalence of automata and economic forms along with the advantages of the cellular-automaton framework in representing structural detail suggests ways in which economic materials may be amalgamated with materials

in the sociological and anthropological domains. This again is a theme that emanates from heuristic applications of automaton schemes.

These lines have been outlined in the preceding chapters with full stress given to the tentative and conjectural nature of such inquiry. This stress and the accompanying caveats must be reiterated. The author has not tried to disguise his own enthusiasm for the styles of analysis based on the automaton concept, and "potentialities" have been advertised rather shamelessly. Nevertheless, there are some touches of (conservative) realism that should be injected into the discussion at this moment of evaluation. First, it will take some years before there can be reasoned, informed, and full assessment of the technique. This is so because the usefulness and acceptability of the automaton approach—even as a basis for metaphorical conjecture—will depend ultimately on what can be accomplished in empirical and quasi-empirical studies. Such studies will take time; even though a SUR model can be mounted rapidly, full implementation and analysis can not be hurried. Some conjectures are premature since the empirical studies are not yet in, but then again the conjectures are needed to prompt the required research. The second main caveat involves recognition that many previous attempts to exploit new methodologies have floundered after what appeared to be strong if not lusty beginnings. Anyone looking for a computer that plays grand-master chess will be aware of this phenomenon. Early investigations show the possibility of making progress; later investigations discover the pitfalls and practical limitations. The first results come too quickly.

Even in the face of these qualifications it should still be useful to sketch out some lines of analysis that appear on the horizon.

Heuristics, Simulation, and Representation

This is the most promising research area, for immediate testing of the technique. Part I of the book outlines representational possibilities in urban economics, development economics, and economic anthropology and suggests model forms. The design of such models is intellectually challenging, as is any attempt to describe interesting societies, groups, and systems. Nevertheless, most economists would possibly wish to evaluate SUR technique or its performance in applications with a substantial policy dimension and where there is an opportunity to fix parameters according to empirical data. On this reasoning, the most fruitful ground for methodological evaluation of SUR would be LDC technology analyses focusing on absorption problems, problems of agricultural innovation, and problems of introducing new industrial techniques. Individual case studies exist—as, for example, in critiques of the "green revolution"—so data availability should not be an issue. No further discussion is required here: the matters are significant and relatively unexplored in standard quantitative analyses.

Complexity Measurement

This is the area that engages the author as an economist, but it is also an area in which it will take a comparatively long time to develop definitive results and an empirical base. The problems which are involved in extending and implementing the analysis outlined in this book are considerable, a few are sketched in the succeeding paragraphs.

(1) *Abstract simulation.* The numerical example given Appendix 3A is barely a first step in a program of identifying critical complexity parameters in theoretical systems and formulating benchmark models which can be used as referents for trade-off analyses of more elaborate systems. Such analyses are required in order to provide a basis for empirical and policy studies.

(2) *Empirical analyses.* The second stage of research into complexity characteristics will involve translating data on physical production systems into automaton formats. This is not difficult conceptually. As noted earlier, engineering data and specifications are frequently in finite-state form, but the task is laborious and judgmental factors abound. This stage of work is in many respects equivalent to the early stages of data experimentation in the development of input-output models.

(3) *Technology analyses.* The first positive results are likely to come from historical analyses of technical change and the development of techniques. Ideally one would be able to develop historical SUR models for a number of goods which have unchanged physical attributes in the final-product market but which have undergone substantial changes in manufacturing method (e.g., textiles, ferrous metals, printed pages, and others). Hopefully, it might turn out that a significant proportion of the technological advance can be isolated and identified with specific system-complexity parameters (e.g., with communication, organizational complexity, or others).

(4) *Capital theoretical analyses.* To the extent that (3) can be accomplished, one obtains important information on which to refine the theory of technical change and theory involving heterogeneous capital. Such analyses would clearly be informative in the development of abstract planning models as well.

(5) *Technical forecasting.* Results bearing on policy are not likely to emerge before stages (1) to (4) are well advanced. The area which appears to be most promising is that of forecasting trends in technology and manufacturing structure.[a] For example, if one examines highly sophisticated contemporary

---

[a]A case can be made that the most sophisticated of this genre is the study by E. Hudson and D. Jorgenson "U.S. Energy, Policy and Economic Growth, 1975-2000" in the *Bell Journal of Economics and Management Science*, Autumn, 1974. The paper amalgamates a dynamic input-output model with econometric sectoral-demand formulations—pricing relationships obtained in one model feed back to alter the parameters in the other. It seems that SUR can usefully supplement this type of mixed-model analysis in exactly the areas where a treatment such as that of Hudson and Jorgenson is weakest. Historical analysis such as that suggested in Chapters 3 and 4 can be used to identify adoptive patterns in infrastructural investment at the microlevel, and it is just these factors which make up to profound alterations in energy use patterns.

As noted in the Appendix to the Introduction and at various points in Chapters 1 and 2, an input-output model is itself an automaton, and the blending of an econometric model with a SUR model is formally equivalent to the blending of an econometric model with an activity-analysis component. It appears feasible, therefore, to develop a model with the Hudson-Jorgenson scheme at its core, but with an amalgamated SUR component used to trace microadaptations and technical trends.

analyses of technical futures such as those developed for projecting energy uses, one finds that projections of the pattern of manufacturing development are largely formed through simple trend extrapolations without a prior theory of manufacturing structure. The explicit complexity-measurement approach points toward direct analysis of the form of technical change and associated endogenous adaptations. Again such results (if they can be obtained) are years away; and there is little point in elaborating these conjectures.

Pure Theory

Chapters 5 to 7 of this book have pointed toward a number of unusual theoretical lines along with conjectures in pure theory relating to general equilibrium, planning, and social choice. To be realistic, these lines must be evaluated as secondary in significance to empirically-based policy analyses. The metaphorical use of automaton analyses drawn from other disciplines produces some immediate insights, but the applicability and acceptability of findings of this sort again will depend ultimately upon the empirical and policy record SUR makes for itself.

The Political Economy of SUR

As we have been told repeatedly, there is no such thing as an apolitical social science or an apolitical social science methodology—even formal and quantitative techniques may serve as apologetics or as revolutionary statements. Nonetheless I frankly find myself unable to make a political assessment of the analysis in this book, although I have the feeling that the approach does engage a number of areas of discipline controversy in political economy.

Part of the problem of political assessment may be that automata-based techniques are highly general and applicable to a wide variety of discipline issues. Thus, at early stages of the research, I found applicable examples in production problems of an essentially neoclassical cast, capital-measurement problems with both Cambridge and neo-Austrian overtones, pure planning problems, and problems in pluralistic political theory. The analysis here of development sequences was suggestive of problems in historical Marxism and also of contemporary problems of structuralism in anthropology and sociology. It is even possible that the faceless and cultureless "smallest units" who are the subject of the book may have class-consciousness which has not yet come to light. In short, the interpretations are for the reader.

Bibliography

Bibliography

Albin, P.S., "Poverty, Education and Unbalanced Economic Growth." *Quarterly Journal of Economics*, February 1970.

_____ , *Social Dimensions of Economic Growth MS*, New York: Basic Books, 1975.

_____ , "Uncertainty Information Exchange and the Theory of Indicative Planning," *Economic Journal*, March 1971, pp. 61-80.

Arrow, K.J., *Social Choice and Individual Values*, New York: Wiley, 1963.

Arrow, K.J., and G. Debreu, "Existence of an Equilibrium for a Competitive Economy," *Econometrica*, 22, 1954.

Beckman, M., *Location Theory*, New York: Random House, 1968.

Böhm-Bawerk, E. von, *Positive Theory of Capital*, 1891.

Burks, A.W. (ed.), *Essays on Cellular Automata*, Urbana, Ill.: University of Illinois, 1970.

Burmeister, E., "A Review and Synthesis of the Neo-Austrian and Alternate Approaches to Capital Theory," manuscript, University of Pennsylvania Working Paper, 1974.

Campbell, D.E., "Social Choice and Intensity of Preference," *Journal of Political Economy*, 81 (1), January/February 1973.

Codd, E.F., *Cellular Automata*, New York: Academic Press, 1968.

Gale, D., *Theory of Linear Economic Models*, New York: McGraw-Hill, 1960.

Gecseg, F., and I. Peak, *Algebraic Theory of Automata*, Budapest: Akademiai Kiado, 1972.

Ginsburg, A., *Algebraic Theory of Automata*, New York: Academic Press, 1968.

Hicks, J.R., *Capital and Time: A Neo-Austrian Theory*, New York: Oxford, 1973.

_____ , *A Theory of Economic History*, New York: Oxford, 1973.

Hudson, E., and D. Jorgenson, "U.S. Energy Policy and Economic Growth, 1975-2000," *Bell Journal of Economics and Management Science*, Fall 1974.

Hurwicz, L., "On the Concept and Possibility of Informational Decentralization," *American Economic Review*, May 1969.

Jacobs, J., *The Economy of Cities*, New York: Vintage, 1970.

Kindleberger, C., *Economic Development*, New York: McGraw-Hill, 1965.

Levi-Strauss, C., *Structural Anthropology*, Harmondsworth, England: Penguin Books, 1972.

McNaughton, R., "On Nets Made Up of Badly-Timed Elements . . ." (Mimeo) Philadelphia: University of Pennsylvania, 1961b.

_____ , "The Theory of Automata and Survey" in *Advances in Computers*, 2, New York: Academic Press, 1961a.

Minsky, M., *Computation, Finite and Infinite Machines*, Englewood Cliffs, N.J.: Prentice Hall, 1967.

Morgenstern, O, "The Compressibility of Economic Systems and the Problem of Economic Constants," *Zeitschift fur Nazionalokonomie*, XXVI: 1-3 (1966).

Morishima, M., *Theory of Economic Growth*, New York: Oxford, 1969.

Nelson, R.J., *Introduction to Automata*, New York: Wiley, 1968.

Piccoli, M.L., "An Application of Formal Language and Automata Theory to Social Choice," Paper presented to the Econometric Society, December 1973.

Rabin, M., "Probabilistic Automata," *Information and Control*, 6, 1963.

Robinson, J. *The Accumulation of Capital*, New York: Macmillan, 1956.

Ruggles, N., and R. Ruggles, "A Strategy for Merging and Matching Micro Data Sets," National Bureau of Economic Research Workshop, Williamsburg, Virginia, 1973.

Schelling, T., "The Process of Residential Segregation: Neighborhood Tipping," in A. Pascal (ed.), *Racial Discrimination in American Life*, Lexington, Mass.: D.C. Heath, 1972.

Sen, A.K., *Collective Choice and Social Welfare*, San Francisco: Holden-Day, 1970.

Shannon, C., "Computers and Automata," *Proceedings of the IRE*, 1953.

Smith, A., *The Wealth of Nations*, Chicago: Irwin, 1963.

Smith, A.R., "Cellular Automata Complexity TRADE OFFS," *Information and Control*, 1971.

_____ , "Simple Computation-Universal Cellular Spaces," *Journal of the Association for Computing Machinery*, July 1971b.

"The Limits to Growth," Report to the Club of Rome's project on the predicament of mankind, New York: Universe, 1973.

Vandell, K., and Harrison, B., "A Simulation Model of the Ghetto Expansion Process," MS., M.I.T., 1974.

von Neumann, J., "Probabilistic Logics and the Synthesis of Reliable Organisms from Unreliable Components," in Shannon and McCarthy (eds.), *Automata Studies*, Princeton, N.J.: Princeton University Press, 1956.

_____ , *Theory of Self-Reproducing Automata*, (A.W. Burks, ed.), Urbana, Ill.: University of Illinois, 1966.

Weissacker, V., *Steady State Capital Theory*, Berlin, New York: Springer-Verlag, Lecture Notes #54, 1971.

Wolff, E., "Social and Demographic Factors in the Distribution of Occupational Earnings," International Association for Research in Income and Wealth, Rio de Janeiro, 1974 (Second Latin American Conference).

Zeuthen, F., *Economic Theory and Method*, Cambridge, Mass.: Harvard University Press, 1955.

Index

Index

activity analysis. *See* input-output
aggregation, 37, 46, 70-71, 83
Albin, P., 100, 127n
anthropology and ethnography. *See* preindustrial economy
Arrow-Debreu Model, 26
Arrow, K., 128-129, 134-135
Asimov, I., 95n
automata: concept, 1, 11-18; definition, 12; primitive, 14. *See also* cellular automata; neuron; turing machine

Bergson, A., 135
boundary characteristics, 76, 112
bureaucracy, 72
Burks, A., xv, 70, 109, 110n, 134

Campbell, D., 128, 129n, 130
capital theory, 4, 44-45, 67, 95-103 *passim*, 141, 142
cellular automata: concept, 1-10 *passim*, 11, 18-23, 25; definition of, 20, 22, 75-76; Moore form, 85-86; simulation models, 35-50 *passim*; structural models, 67-88; systems, 127-130, 139; uniform laminar hierarchic (ULHS), 76-88; Von Neuman form, 85-87, 109-111. *See also* "Garden of Eden" theorem, "Self-Reproduction" theorem
cellular space. *See* cellular automaton
choice theory, 10, 23, 108, 127-138
cities and urban simulation, 58-60, 111-113. *See also* complexity, urbanization and
Codd, E.F., 70, 110n
colonial dependence, 113, 125
compensation principle, 128
complexity: concept of, 3-6, 10, 109-110; infrastructure and, 3, 6, 13, 83, 94, 95, 101-103, 111-113; measurement of, 5-8, 22, 25; numerical calculation of, 69-94, 95-103 *passim*, 139-142; organization and, 6, 25, 45, 95, 97, 142; technical change and, 3, 6, 73, 83, 94, 95-103 *passim*; tradeoffs, 69-71

computation universality, 26-29, 70
computers, 1-10 *passim*, 14, 24-25, 73-74, 109-110, 140
congestion. *See* externalities
Conway, R., 51
cost of capital, 99-102

decision rule, 127
decomposition of models, 48, 83. *See also* aggregation
demographic models, 36-42, 56-57, 83, 115
dialectic sequences, 76, 88
Dore, C., 55
dynamics, 48-49, 68, 76, 84-85, 114

economics data, 37, 45
economic development: absorption of technology, 102-108, 125; and models, 6, 55, 95, 102-105, 112, 140
equilibrium concepts, 21, 28-29, 48-49, 98, 122-128, 133, 139
externalities, 95, 121-125, 139

finite state device. See automata and cellular automata
flow of funds, 5

"game of life", xv, 9, 36, 51-54, 113, 115-116
"garden of eden" theorem, 107, 113-114, 139
Gardner, M., xv, 51
Gödel, K., 108, 127, 134, 137
golden age growth, 100

halting problem, 26-29, 127-138 *passim*
Hicks, J., 128
hierarchy. *See* complexity and organization; production organization of
Hoggatt, A., 55
Holland, J., 10
Hudson, E., 141
Hurwicz, L., 127n

information exchange, 127

149

About the Author

Peter S. Albin teaches economics at New York University and at John Jay College of the City University of New York. He has also taught at Cambridge University and at Berkeley. A graduate of Yale University, he received the Ph.D. in economics from Princeton University. Professor Albin has written widely on growth and capital theory, planning, economics of uncertainty, poverty, and income distribution. His articles have appeared in the *American Economic Review, The Quarterly Journal of Economics, the Economic Journal, Kyklos, The Journal of Finance, The Southern Economic Journal*, and other scholarly journals.